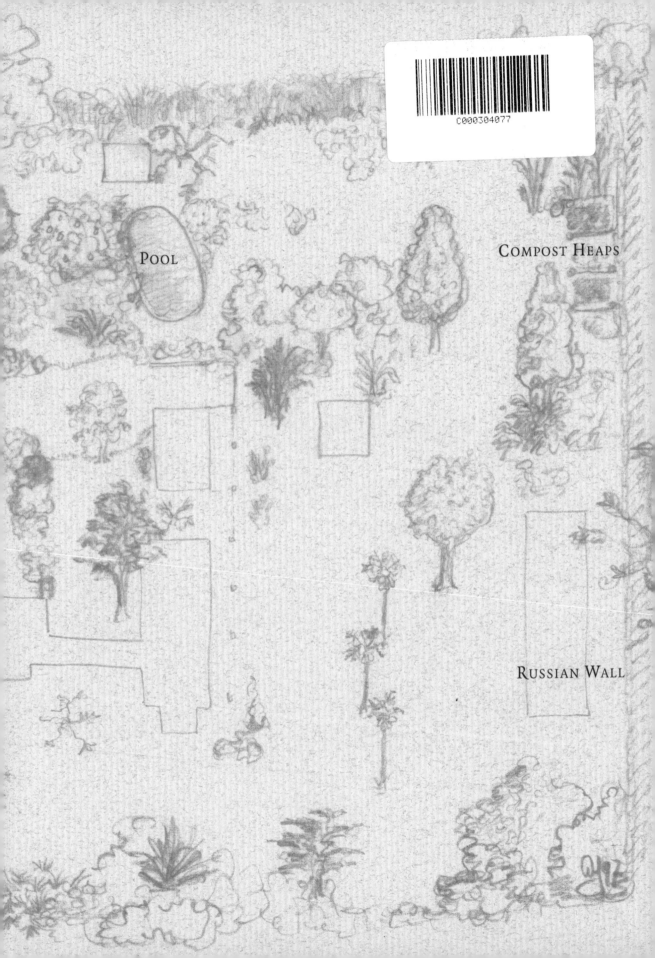

POOL

COMPOST HEAPS

RUSSIAN WALL

# TWO FIVE NINE

## REMINISCENCES FROM A GARDEN OFF JALAN AMPANG

by PETER JENKINS

CIP Data
Jenkins, Peter John Laidlow
Two Five Nine,
    reminiscences from a garden off Jalan Ampang
by Peter Jenkins
Bibliography p. 95-104
Includes index

ISBN 983-99274-0-x

1. Gardens-Kuala Lumpur-Styles 2. Gardens-Kuala
Lumpur-Design 3. Plants-Ornamental 4. Gardening
I. Title
635.09595116

Marianne North illustrations with kind permission from
the Royal Botanical Gardens, Kew
Woodcuts by Carola Colley
Chapter end illustrations by Waveney Jenkins
Cover photographs by Ton van Bragt

Graphic design by Design Team, Kuala Lumpur

Colour separation by Tye Cine
Printing by Atlas Cetak

# Author's Note

Special thanks to Waveney, Anna and Cheng Hong for their invaluable encouragement, advice and help; and also to Shirley for patiently doing all the typing.

343    **Foliage and Flowers of the Flamboyante at Singapore**
(This is presumably a Delonix Regia)

# CONTENTS

# THE REALLY IGNORANT BEGINNER (RIB)

 "In America only the successful writer is important, in France all writers are important, in England no writer is important, and in Australia you have to explain what writing is", so said an American in 1961. Almost exactly 300 years earlier Moliere commented "I always do the first line well, but I have trouble doing the others".

This book is being written in Malaysia, not a land famous for its writers and I can say truthfully that the first four lines were extremely simple because I did not compose them myself. Indeed, it is the rest of the book which is going to cause the problem.

But let me be honest. The problem does not lie with me in writing the book; it is much more likely to lie with you in reading it unless you happen to be one of those few people who share my interest in simple gardening in Malaysia.

In short, this book is an indulgence.

At the age of 52, having then been living in Kuala Lumpur for 26 years, and until then having experienced difficulty differentiating between a daffodil and a dandelion, for various reasons I quite suddenly became involved with the garden. This should not have been a surprise, even if it was. Firstly my mother has built an unusual and now quite famous garden

608    **The Avocado or Alligator Pear**                                      9
         "Persea Gratissima is a member of the Laurel family, native of tropical America.
         The moth is Tropeae Selene"

in East Anglia in Britain. Secondly, we had since 1976 been living in an attractive bungalow just off Ampang Road in Kuala Lumpur, set in about one and half acres of garden. The bungalow is owned by the Rubber Research Institute of Malaysia, and was built along with a number of similar houses in the area in the 1930's. These houses were lived in by RRI staff, most of them boffins, and many of them no doubt responsible for getting Malaya's rubber on to the world market, and therefore major contributors to the welfare and development of the country.

I have not troubled the RRI to find out who our predecessors in 259, Jalan Ampang were, but sometime I will. In particular, I would like to find out who was responsible for planting some of the larger trees which feature in this book.

Regardless of those two factors, between 1976 and 1988, it was my wife and our kebun Subbiah who were the architect and contractor respectively for the development of the Garden at 259. What then caused the great change?

In the latter respect, I believe there were three direct factors and one indirect.

Firstly in 1988, John Skrine who had spent most of his life in Malaya/Malaysia, and amongst other things had founded the law firm, Skrine & Co., one of the top three legal firms in the country, started to think about retiring and returning to live full time in his attractive fortified Manor House in County Wexford in Ireland. John was a war-time soldier with the 7th Hussars, with whom he had won an MC in Italy, and as well as horses, and of course the law, shrubs and trees featured strongly among his interests. In 1988 John started his retirement process which meant about 6 months in Ireland and two or three visits a year comprising 6 months in Kuala Lumpur as a consultant to Skrine & Co. With our children at school or university or in employment in Britain, there was accommodation available at 259 for John Skrine.

I recall him saying to me shortly after he moved in "you've got quite a decent sort of garden here, why don't you grow a few trees?" I was mildly irritated by this as up to then, I had always considered that we already had a large number of trees in the garden, some of which were really quite big. Nevertheless at intervals during the next few months, John would turn up with the odd pot containing some feeble looking specimen, with a name which I always had difficulty in recalling. Subbiah did his best; some of them survived; some of them did not.

On another of his visits I recall John saying "you know, you've got quite a big garden here, you ought to make a bit of compost". Of course I knew what compost was; there was plenty of it made at my parents' house in East Anglia. Again, I was mildly irritated as I had more than enough to think about running the International Chamber of Commerce in Kuala Lumpur, and anyway, how the devil do you start to make compost? Then a second and much more traumatic event took place; and here I have to make a little digression. Ever since I can remember, in the cricket season, and as far as cricket goes the same months in Malaysia are allocated to the cricket season as in Britain, I had spent in my view an entirely acceptable amount of time playing cricket. When I arrived in Malaya in early 1962, I continued to take the game quite seriously, although I do recall being in disgrace for turning up late for a State trial one Sunday morning, through having misjudged the time it took to get back from an early morning session of snipe shooting near Sungei Buloh. After a few years of the serious stuff, I then with much relief enrolled myself in the Selangor Club Saturday side which used to turn out every Saturday afternoon on the Padang through the season. The side comprised players of varying ages, most of whom had played reasonably good cricket. For 12 years over the '70s, the side was captained by Norman Wood, the then senior partner of

Price Waterhouse, who used to rule the event with a rod of iron. Batsmen were expected to bat and get on with it; all bowlers were given an approximately equal number of overs; the first batting side was expected to declare at tea time; and players were expected to be reasonably well turned out. It was extraordinary how many runs were scored in this 4-hour game, often over 300 in the afternoon, and there was nearly always an exciting finish shortly before 6.30 p.m. when stumps were drawn.

The famous Lall Singh, Malaysia's only citizen to have played test cricket (India, before World War II), used to look after the ground, and there was always a good wicket and a well kept outfield. Norman Wood retired to England, and Lall Singh went on to the great pavilion, but the excellent cricket on the Padang on Saturday afternoon continued.

For those of you not familiar with Kuala Lumpur, the Padang (field) is that area in the middle of the city surrounded by the original Secretariat buildings to the south, the original Chartered Bank building to the west, St. Mary's Church to the east, and the Selangor Club, (now Royal) or the Dog as it has always been known, to the north.

The Padang is state land but had been leased to the Selangor Club which had looked after it since 1887 and used it for playing soccer, hockey, rugby, tennis and cricket. The Padang has always been unfenced and open for the citizens of Kuala Lumpur to stroll about on in the evening and when games were not in progress. Not many playing fields could be said to have been so heavily used. At the same time, apart from in Singapore where there is a similar Padang, no other capital city in the world could boast a similar "village green" in the middle of the metropolis.

To most lovers of Kuala Lumpur the news in early 1988 that the Padang was to be dug up to provide an underground car park and shopping facilities, and a concrete "parade ground" to enable the annual independence celebrations to be appropriately carried out, came as an appalling shock. Following considerable outcry, the design was changed to accommodate grass rather than concrete, albeit on a much reduced area. Three years later cricket was back on the Padang, and on 14 July 1991 (Bastille Day) I was given the honour of facing the first ball on the new composite wicket. The wicket is excellent, but the leg and offside boundaries need extending a further 30 yards to ensure that visiting sides will want to visit K.L. again.

If you are a cricketer you will appreciate that playing on bad wickets becomes increasingly unattractive as you get older; and compared with the Padang, most Kuala Lumpur wickets are bad. I therefore decided to give up cricket during the time that the Padang was out of commission, and that decision was made at about the same time as John Skrine's suggestions about making compost.

It was also at about this time on a visit to my tailor, Kwong Fook Wing (Established 1915, Tailor, by appointment to HRH Almarhum Sultan Ismail Nasiruddin Shah of Trengganu), Mr Kwong commented "so we seem to have put on a little weight since we last saw us haven't we". I disputed the matter but he may have been right.

So three incidents highlighted the problem, and getting involved in a small garden off Ampang Road provided a solution. But I think there is another factor which we all come to appreciate as we soldier on, if we are lucky enough to pass our 50th year, and that is that we all tend to become a little less aggressive. We tend to start playing games for the enjoyment of playing them rather than to win. We tend to stop shooting things with guns and start shooting them with cameras. We tend to be more sympathetic to peaceful solutions, however military we may have been in the past. We tend to become interested, if not even astonished, at the way things grow. And it is this astonishment which is I believe the root cause of the fascination which an involvement with a garden provides.

If you have read this far I think you will then have some idea what the next few chapters are not. They are not going to be a series of instructions about what you should do and what you should not do to build a magnificent garden. "Gardening in the Lowlands of Malaya" by R E Holttum, "Living with Plants" by Amy and John Ede, "Malaysian Flowers in Colour" by Professor H F Chin, "Wayside Trees of Malaya" by Professor E J H Corner, "Tropical Gardening and Planting" by H F MacMillan, "Gardening in Malaya" by E St Clair-Morford, "Some Common Trees of Malaya" by Betty Molesworth Allen, and "The Tropical Garden City" by Dr Salleh Mohd Noor, Wong Yew Kwan and Dr F S P Ng are just some of the books you need if it is advice and instruction that you are seeking. You will also no doubt study Lam Peng Sam's regular advice in the New Straits Times. These experts will be quoted in this book on numerous occasions, and this should be treated as my note of acknowledgement of, and gratitude for the expertise of those authors.

What you will find are some comments from an enthusiastic amateur which may be of some help to the Really Ignorant Beginner (RIB); and it is to the RIB to whom this book is directed. There are also a number of illustrations. The woodcuts are by my daughter, Carola Colley, who is now an artist living in the Isle of Man, and the black and white pencil sketches are by my wife, Waveney.

There are also reproductions of the paintings of Marianne North, that astonishing Victorian lady (1830-1890) who travelled round the world on a number of occasions producing a huge number of outstandingly magnificent oil paintings of botanical items. Towards the end of her life, she built a gallery at the Royal Botanic Gardens at Kew to house her collection of paintings, 832 in number, and today the gallery is a must for any visitor to London remotely interested in tropical trees and plants. The reproductions have been arranged with the kind permission of the Royal

Botanic Gardens, and I was most grateful for the assistance of Nicholas Martland of the Library at Kew in this context. The numbers, titles and descriptions under the reproductions are extracts from the "Official Guide to the North Gallery, Royal Gardens, Kew" - 6th Edition 1914 - Price Six Pence.

My father had a cousin who served for many years in India and wrote a magnificent little book called "Past Imperative". Friends rebuked him for not including amongst the fascinating information in the book sufficient trivial details, domestic and professional, about the life he was living at the time. What was the cost of a pound of butter, a loaf of bread, a pint of beer? Where did you buy your shoes? What happened if you got appendicitis? Such things provide fascinating reading for later generations. I hope to err in the opposite direction, and if I do not provide a substantial element of totally trivial information, it will not be for want of trying.

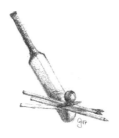

# JALAN AMPANG

# 2

Someone once said that a mine is a hole in the ground owned by a liar. I do not know whether he was referring specifically to a Malayan tin mine. But I do know that I would not have liked to have been a Chinese tin miner in the 1850's in Selangor. Having arrived by sea from China probably via Singapore at Pengkalan Batu, now the town of Port Klang, you got into a small boat with all your tools, kit and food and spent a few days poling up the winding River Klang until you reached the junction (Kuala) where the River Gombak joins the River Klang. At this point you clambered off your boat onto a muddy embankment (benteng), an area today officially named Benteng, which now provides a site for three buildings for international banks, namely Standard Chartered, the Hongkong Bank and Citibank.

You then moved off down a jungle path for about 7 miles and you came to a place called Ampang, so called because of the dams (ampang) constructed there by the tin miners. This jungle track was eventually to become Jalan Ampang or Ampang Road. Some of those miners survived and made some money. Most of them didn't. A few fell prey to tigers, but the vast majority succumbed to the malarial mosquitoes which thrived in the stagnant waters of the mining pools.

305   **The Gool-Achin or Caracucha (Frangipani)**
"... known as Plumeria Acutifolia"

However a sufficient number survived to ensure that Kuala Lumpur, a remote village in the 1850's, flourished to become the state capital in 1880 and the federal capital in 1896.

About forty years later, the Rubber Research Institute was allocated land and built a number of houses at a point about halfway between Benteng and the village that was now called Ampang; Jalan Ampang had become then, and is now, the most well known road in Kuala Lumpur. Most of the biggest houses nearer to Benteng are no longer with us having been knocked down to be replaced by the universal office block. On the other hand, many of the less grand houses remain and long may they do so. If they don't, it will not be for lack of endeavour by the hardworking and enormously successful Heritage Trust of Malaysia which since its founding in 1984 has saved so many buildings from the bulldozer.

Of the houses built in the 1930's very few remain, one of which is 259, Jalan Ampang.

259 stands on about 1.5 acres of flat land. The building is a typical "between-the-wars" one-storey bungalow type house - high ceilings, hard wood small pane casement windows, terrazzo floors, steep tile roof with a five foot overhang, and two bedrooms and bathrooms. The two bedroom concept was almost universal for town and plantation houses for expatriates until the 1960's when expatriate requirements resulted in a proliferation of three or four bedroom, low ceiling, air-conditioned accommodation.

This house stands in a small garden. "Comparisons is odious" said Mr Micawber. By Carcosa standards, the 259 garden is small, but compared with almost any other garden in Kuala Lumpur, it is in fact quite large. I should explain that Carcosa is the earliest really substantial house in Kuala Lumpur. It was presented to the British Government by Malaysia's first Prime Minister, Tunku Abdul Rahman Putra, as a token of

Witch's Tongue - Clerodendron Macrosiphon

the nation's gratitude to Britain for assistance in the 1947-59 Emergency, was until recently the residence of the British High Commissioner, and is now an hotel.

Unlike some of the sites further down Jalan Ampang which are founded on tin tailings, 259 is based on the standard Malay clay soil prevalent throughout the country. This soil consists of laterite which as the Edes say "is the most intractable form of heavy clay", the word being derived from "later", the latin word for a "brick". The Edes go on to say "laterite is orange-brown in colour, baked hard when dry and a gluey mess when wet, acidic in content, and lacking in aeration. It is the task of the gardener to turn this unpromising material into the rich, dark brown and crumbly loam which will enable our plants to thrive".

Here we have a small disgression. In the paragraph above I refer to "tin tailings". Tin tailings comprise the worked out earth that is left following a tin mining operation and require major attention before anything will grow on them. Tin tailings also provide a problem in that they appear to attract lightning, possibly because of the residual tin element. My father who was in Malaysia for a brief spell in 1934 had three major memories.

His first, a most pleasant one, was of many hours exercising the numerous horses of Tunku Abu Bakar, the brother of the then Sultan of Johor. His second was centred on a motor car journey from Singapore to Penang in one of the first Morris Minors in Malaya. The entry into Kuala Lumpur was not mentioned; nor for that matter into Ipoh. However, the episode that stuck in his memory took place 15 or so miles short of Ipoh where two of the car's tyres blew out. The spare wheel sorted out one problem. The second was solved by stuffing the tyre with grass, and the vehicle moved forward again towards Ipoh. At the same time however a classic late afternoon thunderstorm developed with the usual bucketing rain and lightning dancing among the tin bearing earth along the road side. The grass in the tyre soon heated up and both the tyre and grass began to smoke and smell; the lightning became continuous; and my father thought that he was finished.

My father did successfully continue his journey to Penang where he got rid of the car, and then to the scene of his third memory. It was the end of his five year tour in the Far East and he had boarded the ship to take him back to England for his leave. Just before the vessel departed an elderly Malay lady sold him a Malay Kris, and having done so and presumably being satisfied with the bargain, proceeded at no extra charge to tell him his fortune. "You will" she said, "return to your home country, which you will not leave for twenty years". As my father was expecting to come back to his job in the Far East after his leave, this was not the news he was expecting, nor in fact wanted. Nevertheless, he found a home posting waiting for him on his return to England, and despite no less than four embarkation orders during World War II, he did not leave England until he visited Nigeria twenty years later. In the meantime the Kris has not been entirely decorative. In 1962 it functioned to cut our wedding cake, and in 1995 it made itself useful again for my son Mark when he married Ellie Ling.

On that note we will close this chapter before we contemplate the various steps to be taken to enable even the most determined plant to exhibit some growth when it is stuck into this great sea of laterite.

# Dealing with Laterite

3

Every now and again you meet people who tell you they have got "green fingers". The implication is that everything which they touch turns to green, blossom and fruit, and this is all due to some magical quality. Certainly the element of magic is something which tends to be promoted, and I have never heard of anyone from the so-called "green fingered" brigade do much to contradict that assessment.

I personally do not go along with this magic theory. Lots of us like to see things growing nicely and producing attractive leaves and flowers and fruit, and I suppose it is easy to be a little bit conned by those people who successfully organise their gardens to do so. In fact, you usually find that those people who have a so-called "feel" for the soil are those people who spent their formative years i.e. up to the age of approximately 9, either in the country or surrounded by a reasonably well cared for garden. At that age, whether you like it or not, you absorb how things are done. You develop an affinity for plants. Without realising it, you get an instinct for the sort of environment that a plant needs to survive. Does it want sunshine or shade? A damp or dry location? A clay or humus soil? If you can answer such questions in the context of a very small number of plants, shrubs and trees, you can quite easily pass yourself off as an expert.

488   **Mandrinette and mountain home of the Pitcher Plant in the Distance**   23
"... the showy shrub here represented is Hibiscus liliiflorus, Cav., a native of Mauritius ..." (This looks identical to our Hibiscus Rosa-Sinensis)

In summary, I am delighted to acknowledge that a number of my friends have "green fingers". I do not however accept that they have magical qualities. I merely accede that they are at least one step ahead of me, and in that context I consider that their brains are ruthlessly to be picked.

Where then do these "green fingered" experts succeed spectacularly? If they are to succeed at all, it must primarily be in the area of comprehension of the soil, and what grows in what. Here again, as far as I can see, and no doubt real experts will shoot me down for over simplification, the Malaysian soil problem is not usually a difficult one to solve.

I have glanced through several books on soil in the context of Kuala Lumpur gardening problems, and for the RIB* there are two books particularly worth studying. When it comes to reading, gardeners have a short span of concentration, and so the first book recommended is "Gardening in Malaya" by E St. Clair-Morford, Pages 2 to 7 - the pages are very small.

The second is "Living with Plants" by Amy and John Ede, Pages 6 and 7 - the pages are larger but the RIB should not be put off because there is a substantial illustration on each page.

St. Clair-Morford was writing in 1926 and Amy and John Ede 54 years later in 1980. Things don't seem to have changed very much, thank the Lord, and much of the advice is very similar; and Rule One is clearly "there is no point in thinking about planting anything anywhere until there is an understanding about the soil".

As we mentioned in Chapter Two, in most of Malaysia and certainly in Kuala Lumpur, the average soil consists of clay or laterite. There we read the Ede's definition of laterite. The Oxford Dictionary defines laterite in similarly dispiriting terms as "a red friable ferruginous surface clay much used for road making in the tropics".

Surveying a great area of laterite, the RIB may easily become

* Really Ignorant Beginner

Scarlet Passion Flower - Passiflora Coccinea

dismayed; particularly if he knows that clay soil is heavy, and often wet, and must be lightened by "deep chungkoling" and the addition of sand and organic substances. Clay soils are rich in plant food but require "cultivation to render them fertile". Not very difficult to understand; however someone has to do the "deep chungkoling", someone has to find the sand, and someone has to arrange for the organic substances.

So let us assume that you, or your kebun, or your contractor has undertaken the "deep chungkoling". Not difficult, and provided you are reasonably fit as an exercise it is indeed excellent for reducing your waistline. Incidentally a chungkol is a tool rather like the English pick, but with a spade head instead of a spike, and the only implement to dig a hole with in laterite soil. Local spades are more like an English shovel, and local forks are very feeble. Currently imported German forks at about RM 94.00 each are therefore worth buying.

Secondly, the sand problem is not a difficult one, merely a question of finding someone to deliver a lorry load of river sand (not salt sand), and this will keep you going for years.

Thirdly, and most vital is "the organic substances". Organic substances, or decayed organic matter, produces humus, the black earthy substance in the soil. Humus soils are always rich, often too rich. The addition of lime and deep chungkoling will let in the air and make it fertile. The ideal top soil in which we can plant things, comprises the right mixture of laterite (clay) and lime and humus. The resultant mixture will you hope produce the right composition of nitrogen, phosphorus, potash and magnesium, as well as the numerous other trace elements that ordinary people don't know about, that combine to make things grow.

How much clay should be mixed and how much humus, and how much lime should be thrown in? There are plenty of experts who will give you differing information. In the meantime, why not try about 50%

humus, 50% clay, two handfuls of lime and two or three spades of sand to a barrow load. If it works you can tell everyone you have "green fingers". If it doesn't you can either call in the experts, or experiment until it does.

But let us look at some of the practical problems. Your laterite is there in hyper abundance; your lime (calcium carbonate) you can buy a bagful of anywhere. It is your humus, or "decayed organic matter" which is your key to success, and which as far as I can see, is only obtained in one sensible way, and that is by the manufacture in your own garden of compost. Let us devote Chapter Four to compost.

# Making Compost

4

Compost is the result of the disintegration of vegetable waste by means of fermentation into a material similar to cattle manure. The resulting concoction is, or so they say, as good as if not better than the best cattle manure.

It may or may not contain the necessary amount of nitrogen, phosphorus, potash and magnesium. If it doesn't, you will soon find out and make the necessary additions when spreading your compost strategically amongst your trees, shrubs and plants. I think most people have a general idea as to what compost is, and how to manufacture it. For the RIB in simple terms, you collect all your non-timber garden waste material, grass cuttings, leaves, vegetable waste from the kitchen etc. and pile them together in a heap. Many people will give you different advice about adding in chicken manure, wood ash, lime etc. at different levels, and turning the heap at varying frequencies. There are more ways of killing a cockroach than stuffing it with moth balls.

Basically in Malaysia nature manufactures compost pretty quickly whatever you do or don't do to your heap, and whatever you add or don't add. Nevertheless keeping it aerated by regular turning, together with the addition of a little bit of lime from time to time, no doubt accelerates matters.

I personally make compost on a four-month cycle. I have four 4 foot x 4 foot bays, each divided by chicken netting against a back-up brick wall. Bay 1 collects all the garden's non-woody rubbish during Month 1, and at the end of the month by when the heap is 3 foot or 4 foot high, the contents of Bay 3 are turned into Bay 4, Bay 2 into Bay 3, and Bay 1 into Bay 2. The product in Bay 4 by now is compost and is ready for use. It will be used up during the course of the month in the garden, leaving Bay 4 ready to collect the contents of Bay 3 at the end of the month. The cycle is then repeated. If you are over fifty and reasonably fit, it takes about an hour to turn a heap, and requires only gentle exertion if tackled sensibly.

I am told that in the context of Kuala Lumpur, my compost is stuffed with nitrogen. Phosphorus, if there is any deficiency, is best obtained in Malaysia in the form of rock phosphate; magnesium if there is a shortage can similarly be obtained in the form of magnesium limestone powder; and potash can all be bought from Mr Alex Saw of 25, Jalan Tun H S Lee, Kuala Lumpur.

Thus apart from the lime which you probably will need, and from the phosphorus potash and the magnesium which you probably won't, all your fertiliser is already available in your garden. All that is required is the application of the energy of yourself or that of your kebun to your garden waste. This is then converted into that magnificent dark brown compost which will more than serve the purpose of any humus, and in most circumstances achieve far more than those inorganic fertilisers - with due apologies of course to the international chemical companies - which you now do not have to buy.

There are many recipes for making compost. In particular I like St. Clair-Morford's description. "In India, on the tea estates of Travancore, large composting batteries are maintained and cattle specially kept for the purpose. Some 5 tons of compost yearly per acre are put out among the tea in poor areas. One cow kept at night in a cow shed produces enough manure to make 5 tons of compost a year". I always feel sorry for that cow in Travancore; how embarrassed it must feel when asked by its friends what it does to earn a living.

So much then for a little bit of technology. No doubt it does come in useful from time to time. However, I think it was Dr Johnson who stated that the secret of being a good doctor is to be able to chat up your patient while nature gets on with the healing job. Similarly, I think it can be said that a good gardener wanders around in his garden, while nature gets on with the job of producing his plants.

Torch Ginger

# The Weather and the Seasons

# 5

The average weather forecaster today in Britain is generally a figure of ridicule and contempt with his television maps covered with little clouds, suns, and drops of rain, most of which within 24 hours so often turn out to have been in the wrong place. The same cannot be said of the weather forecaster in Malaysia. "Temperatures in the 80's, generally bright and sunny, with occasional tropical showers later on in the day", will probably enable him to maintain his reputation for excellence for 95 out of every 100 days. Indeed it is true that in Kuala Lumpur there are no seasons and, being only approximately 3 degrees north of the equator, in the course of a year there is only about a 30-minute change in the hours of dawn and dusk. The sun rises in the morning at times varying from 6.56 a.m. to 7.27 a.m. and sets in the evening between 6.56 p.m. and 7.28 p.m. - 1991 times. That magnificent Victorian lady Isabella Bird, travelling in Malaya in 1879, provides in one short page an excellent description of the weather on the West Coast of Malaya, and I have not anywhere read a better one produced in the ensuing 111 years. She writes as follows. "The rainfall is not excessive, averaging about 110 inches annually. And there is no regular rainy season. In fact it rains in moderation all the year round. Three days seldom pass without refreshing showers, and if there are 10

*Morning Glory, Natal*
"Ipomoea Ventricosa, a Mexican species"

Chempaka - Michelia Alba

rainless days together, a rare phenomenon, people begin to talk of "the drought". Practically the year is divided into two parts by the "monsoons". The monsoon is not a storm, as many people suppose from a vague association with the word "typhoon", but a steady wind, blowing in the case of the Malay Peninsula for 6 months from the north east, bringing down the Chinamen in their junks, and for 6 months from the south west, bringing traders from Arabia and India. The climate is the pleasantest during the north east monsoon, which lasts from October to April. It is during the south west monsoon that the heavier rains accompanied by electrical disturbances occur. The central mountain range protects the peninsula alternately from both monsoons, the high Sumatran mountains protecting its west side from the south west winds. The east side is exposed for 6 months to a modified north east monsoon. Everywhere else throughout the almost changeless year, steadily alternating land and sea breezes with gentle variable winds and calms prevail, interrupted occasionally on the

West Coast during the "summer" by squalls from the south west, which last for 1 or 2 hours, and are known as "Sumatras". Hurricanes and earthquakes are unknown. Drenching dews fall on clear nights". She earlier describes the mean annual temperature in Malacca as 80 degrees with a range of 15 degrees, and goes on to state that although the climate is undeniably a hot one, the heat tempered by alternating land and sea breezes is seldom oppressive except just before the rain. So much for the seasons, but often quite a lot of changes take place during the day, if not with the regularity that we used to hear of from seasoned planters - "always rains at 5 o'clock in the afternoon, lasts for an hour, set your watch by it, old boy". Not true now, even if it ever was. Isabella Bird's comments on the weather are still remarkably accurate. The average rainfall is probably a little bit higher now, and certainly in Kuala Lumpur with the massive development that has taken place, the average temperature is probably higher than her 80 degrees. So, having no seasons the gardener's task is simplified. Some things flower all the time; some flower two or three times a year; some drop their leaves two or three times a year and some never. As Miss Bird says, "we tend to call it a drought if we have 10 days without rain", but this seldom seriously affects the garden; although, we do have to be careful then by ensuring that potted plants are regularly watered in the evenings. As far as the gardener is concerned, seasons are not an issue. What is important is that the RJB should try to learn a little bit about the requirements of those individual trees, plants, and shrubs which he wishes to flourish in his garden.

# THE LAYOUT

# 6

There are not many expatriates in Malaysia who do not know Hock Choon Supermarket. Hock Choon has become a legend in its lifetime. 30 years ago when the establishment comprised a small timber structure with a corrugated iron roof, it was generally known in the area as Harrods. Now a substantial two-storey structure, including I am pleased to say Crittall metal windows supplied when I was representing that establishment, and still entirely run by the founding family, Hock Choon Supermarket is famous for three things. Firstly, that it supplies everything that anyone has ever thought of wanting, secondly that its credit management is Herculean in its ferocity, and thirdly that it is the land mark for the lorong (lane) which provides the way into 259, Jalan Ampang.

Going out of Kuala Lumpur along Jalan Ampang, about half way to Ampang Village, you pass Hock Choon Supermarket on your right, and a hundred yards later, immediately after the Esso station, you can turn into the lorong which provides access to six RRI bungalows. If you miss the turning, you come to the Russian Embassy on your right and you have to turn around in the Embassy's gate way - before Glasnost no doubt under the surveyance of a suspicious monitoring device. Having entered the lorong you can see six houses, all notorious in some respects.

611   **Foliage Flowers & Fruit of Vanilla Albida**
"... used to scent and flavour delicate sweet meats and beverages ..."

37

The house opposite 259 is occupied by the Bank Bumiputra Sports Club and provides from time to time many an extraordinary sight. A glimpse of the Bank's ladies tug-of-war team practicing at 8 o'clock in the morning is enough to keep the average man going until lunch time.

The next house comprises an establishment currently run by an attractive couple who sell South East Asian antique furniture. While you are trying to decide what not to buy, they will sell you a good South East Asian meal to help you make your mind up.

Next door No. 255, has seen many tenants in recent years. It used to be occupied by the French Consul whose dogs made almost as much noise as ours.

The house then became a kindergarden for a short time until it was taken over by the colourful Ah Wah, designer, painter, sculptor and chef extraordinaire, together with his partners known as the "Seven Datins". Ah Wah and the Datins converted 255 into the "Tropical Dining Club", the decor of which was designed and carried out by Ah Wah, the furniture designed and made by Ah Wah, and the walls of which were hung floor to ceiling with paintings by Ah Wah. Unfortunately, the partnership did not flourish. Early on a Sunday morning, not too long after the heavily attended opening reception, well featured in Malaysian Tatler, Ah Wah was spied loading all the furniture and pictures on to a lorry, chuckling like a lunatic, clearly having made other arrangements. "The Datins are screwing me", he said and he disappeared down Ampang Road into the early morning mist. 255 is now the Dutch Cottage providing traditional Dutch food to the steadily increasing Dutch community in K.L.

The Russian Wall runs between ourselves and the Embassy compound, a substantial area comprising a dozen or so houses in the past owned by the plantation group Guthries. Purchased by the Russians in the late 1960's the first thing that happened was the erection of an 8 foot

China Star Jasmine or Borneo Pin-Wheel - Tabernaemontana Corymbosa

steel fence. Then, in 1982 when the Russians invaded Afghanistan, certain Muslim elements in Kuala Lumpur took steps to express their hostile views. One such element borrowed a musket from the military, climbed up the steel fence and loosed off a magazine into the Ambassador's residence.

The Ambassador was out to dinner and no one suffered any injury, but as a result of this episode an 8 foot brick wall was erected inside the steel fence. There is in fact another theory on the origin of the wall. The Embassy has a basketball court adjacent to No. 259 on which Embassy officials, who in those days were not allowed out very often, regularly used to exercise themselves. To the significant irritation of the participants my then very small daughter, Tamsin, used to liven up the occasions with ribald commentary, until the wall put a stop to her contributions.

So much for the Russian Wall which provides such an excellent back-up for my 4 bay compost heap. Sharing this wall to the South is the bungalow occupied over the years by a number of good friends. Diana and Bruce Nightingale, from the British Council, were there for a short time and Bruce gives us a kind mention in his recently published autobiography. Martin and Angela Craven were there for rather longer. Martin was a tea-taster and is now a merchant banker, but was more useful to us with his expertise on clocks.

Club Mediterranee were tenants for years, first in the shape of Jacques Seidenberg and Maggie Doyle and later Ben and Lily Bousnina. Although we have new Danish neighbours, also in the antique furniture business, we still think of 257 as French.

Since the 1990's Club Med has developed into an astonishingly successful international organisation providing holidays in exotic places. As the French Foreign Legion has diminished in size so Club Med has grown. Perhaps the same sort of man who used to join the Foreign Legion is now employed by Club Med.

So with a French southern boundary, a Russian eastern boundary, and the lorong comprising the western boundary, the northern boundary until recently, when Sayfol School took it over, was American, in the shape of a bungalow occupied by the Asia Foundation. The Asia Foundation is an American non-profit organisation whose objective is to spread American culture internationally, on the cocktail party circuit usually described as a front for the CIA. Judging from the expansive display of wire, hoops and bits of bent metal strung up above the nearest Russian building, one always assumed it to be the communications centre for the Embassy. We (and the CIA) may of course have been quite wrong. Those items suspended above the building may well have been there for decorative purposes only. My wife is a sculptor and every now and then she produces items comprising wire, hoops and bits of bent metal. Perhaps that Embassy building is the local centre for Soviet sculpture.

We enter the garden from the lorong and for easy reference we have the French quarter on the right, the American quarter on the left, the house ahead of us in the middle of the garden with the servant's quarters, stores and garage behind. The swimming pool area is adjacent to the garage, and the Russian Wall area lies behind.

So these are the five areas on which we can focus when we look at those trees, shrubs and plants which survive and in many cases thrive at 259, Jalan Ampang.

317     **(left)The Chumpa or Chempaka**
"Michelia Chempaka…, fragrance so strong that bees seldom if ever alight on them (Sir W. Jones). This tree is sacred to Vishnu and is therefore an object of superstitious regard on the part of the Hindoos, who adorn their hair with the flowers"

660     **(right) Foliage & Flowers of an Indian Climbing Shrub (Beaumontia)**
"… Beaumontia Grandiflora climbs to the top of the highest trees"

42                         

**East Anglia Garden**
My mother's garden at Pages, Shalford in East Anglia, looking south to the orchard and woods beyond.

# The Swimming Pool Area

7

One sort of logic says that we should begin our commentary through the eyes of a visitor. "On entering through the gates on the left you will see etc. etc." Another sort would be to start with the dawn and note the sort of observations that I have made on so many occasions. We will follow this second option.

Assuming the previous evening has not been too onerous I try to be in the swimming pool by 6.45 a.m. each morning and then complete the task of swimming a quarter of a mile in a decreasingly comatose condition. The pleasure of seeing the Malaysian dawn break, which it does extremely speedily, makes up for the tedium of the operation.

First of all a short word about that mystical half light period, which only lasts for about 15 minutes, between the black of pre-dawn and the bright of early day. This is the time when you see things; and I must relate the details of one of my half light visions.

One evening in the earlier 80's, I came back from the office to find it raining heavily at 259 and upon entering the driveway, I passed a fellow on his way out. As you get older you tend to improve your ability at spotting crooks, and certainly I recall that this character did not look like a church warden.

592   **Two Climbing Shrubs painted at Singapore**
"Quisqualis indica, L. with red and white flowers and Thunbergia erecta, T. Anders"

Anyway, off he went and in I went to be told by my wife the sad story that he had just related. Apparently Subbiah the kebun, whom I have mentioned earlier, had been knocked off his bicycle by a motorcar, badly broken his leg, and been warded at the General Hospital. There was an urgent requirement for a RM 100.00 deposit to get things moving, and Subbiah's friend had just called to see if we could help out. This we did, and would have gone to see Subbiah that evening in hospital had this been possible. We would have been wasting our time.

Next morning as I emerged from the pool after my statutory quarter of a mile, in that mystical half light which we were talking about, whom did I see coming out of the bushes in the American quarter, but Subbiah, as large as life, and with two clearly unbroken legs and laughing most cheerfully. Lazarus risen from the dead. Being charitable I do not believe that Subbiah took a share of the RM 100.00; nevertheless the news had got around mightly quickly and clearly constituted the best Tamil joke of the year.

But that was not the end of the story. About a year later, this time as I was about to leave for the office, an old Indian turned up on the door step and introduced himself as a close friend of Subbiah, who incidentally should have been hard at work somewhere in the garden (his normal hours are from 7.00 a.m. to 9.30 a.m.). The old man was clearly not from the Kuala Lumpur smart set, and he had not been near a sharp razor blade for sometime. Sorry to bother us he said, but his friend Subbiah had been knocked off his bicycle by a motorcar, had a badly broken leg, and had been warded at the General Hospital. A deposit was required, and could we possibly help out. You will understand that this little request did not get an enormously friendly reception. A joke's a joke, but so much for a pantomime I said in my best Malay, and I suggested that he move out of the area with the speed of Wesley Hall with a following wind. But of course I was wrong. Poor Subbiah was in hospital with his leg broken in three places, and to cut a long story short, it did not mend properly until he had spent 6 months back in his home village in South India, where a combination of his two wives and ayurvedic medicine eventually got him back into prime condition. We missed him while he was away; at the time of writing he has been with us for 26 years. Not a great gardener in the European sense, and possibly an army barber by training; armed with a set of garden shears anything in reach is in danger of getting the short back and sides treatment to the extent that he is now only let loose on the bamboo hedge. But excellent at mowing the lawns and with a prodigious strength when any special item needs knocking down or digging up. So much then for the moment for Subbiah.

Now the swimming pool itself is certainly not something to write home about, being one of these above the ground "Clark" jobs which I bought second hand from David Davidson, the retiring Managing Director of Anglo-Oriental Tin when he left K.L. for London in 1976. Moving a pool of this type is a simple matter. This pool though was probably disappointed with the move as the Anglo-Oriental house was then purchased by the Government for the use of the Prime Minister; millions of dollars were spent on it to convert it into something rather more grand than the pool's new home at 259. Installed it has been an excellent investment; not big, only 10 yards long, it has nevertheless provided the family with hundreds of miles of swimming; not beautiful, but it is now concealed on all sides by well established banks of shrubs and trees which camouflage its utilitarian appearance.

### To the North

To the north of the pool stands an ancient Common Frangipani (Plumeria Accuminata named after a 17th Century French botanist

Angel's Trumpet - Randia Macrantha

Charles Plumier). This is probably one of the commonest sights in gardens in India, Sri Lanka and South East Asia, although not a native, and believed to have been imported by the Spaniards into the Philippines from Mexico or some say Peru. There are two types, Accuminata or Rubra with pointed leaves, and the larger Obtusa, sometimes up to 40 foot high with rounded leaves, but otherwise very similar.

Accuminata features with white, yellow, pink or red highly fragrant flowers, while Obtusa only has white flowers with a yellow centre. Most religions seem to find them rather acceptable as they can usually be found around mosques, Buddhist temples, Hindu temples and Christian churches.

In the north the Malays tend to call the Frangipani, and certain other highly fragrant trees, Chempaka to cause further confusion to the RJB. Cut the bark of your Frangipani and white latex will flow, poisonous but we are told only lethal in large quantities. St. Clair-Morford says the Frangipani never seeds in this country - perhaps true in 1926; not true on rare occasions in the 1990s at 259. Our poolside number is also a little bit special because entwined amongst its branches is a Beaumontia Multiflora which two or three times a year produces magnificent chalice shaped white flowers. To date the Frangipani does not seem too concerned at its python-like embrace. MacMillan tells us that the powerful fragrance of the Frangipani closely resembles the Frangipani perfume first distilled by a botanist of the name in the 16th Century.

### To the West

A thick bank of shrubs conceals the pool from the western viewer. Firstly like a sinister sentinel, fifteen foot high, stands a Dracaena Fragrans. Dracaena means dragon and most gardens have three or four different brands of Dracaena. Dracaena Fragrans is only fragrant about once every 8 years in the lowlands, and at 259 we have yet to see it perform.

Here is also a Cordyline Terminalis, a red leafed similarly sinister member of the Dracaena family, and by it a Polyscias (or Panax as it is also known) of which there are numerous varieties; the Malays call the whole lot Puding. Alongside is an Acalypha Godseffiana; Acalyphas like Poly-scias Crotons and Dracaenas seem to flourish with or without much attention in every Malaysian garden. Amongst these thrives an Exocaria whose latex is "blistering to the skin and very damaging or even blinding to the eyes", hence its Malay name Buta Buta. But it owes its popularity to its leaves which are a dramatic dark green on one side and bright red on the other. Then amongst all this lot struggles a Cape Honeysuckle (Tecomaria Capensis) a native of South Africa, which makes up for its scruffy appearance by providing magnificent orange honeysuckle type flowers at frequent intervals.

Arising out of this jungle is a small Avocado Pear tree (Persea Americana). This is a tropical American fruit and although widely grown in Indonesia does not seem to be hugely successful in Malaysia. For 15 years this one claimed the distinction of many local Avocado trees in failing to produce any pears. There are a number of other fruit trees at 259, all of which share this inability to produce fruit, and my excuse has always been that there are insufficient dry periods in the K.L. climate to permit fruit to form. In February 1991, seven fine pears appeared, and the seed of the first one consumed produced another tree, which is growing at speed and which I hope will not take so long to earn its keep.

Finally, to fill in the space up to the garage is a massive Hibiscus Rosa-Sinensis, now about 12 foot high and continually covered with its well known scarlet flowers, that is except when the time comes round for some routine heavy pruning.

The Hibiscus, which originates from China, is the national flower of Malaysia, the Bunga Raya. It is a sensible choice as there are said to be over 300 varieties and hybrids, and this means that Malaysians, who gen-erally are artistically inclined, find it difficult to draw or paint a Hisbiscus which is botanically incorrect. There are ten varieties at 259, but more of these later.

Just behind this barrier lie two further clusters of growth, one to the west and one to the north. The first starts with a young Ceylon Ironwood tree (Mesua Ferrea) which should grow to 60 feet, from its present 12 foot, and in due course provide us with highly scented yellow stamened white blooms. Keeping it company is an ancient Honeysuckle (Lonicera Caprifolium) which never seems to be quite as happy as it would be in England. Nevertheless, its early morning scent is pleasantly nostalgic to any Englishman.

Beside it there is another Hibiscus, the well known Rose of Sharon or Hibiscus Mutabilis. Mutabilis because its substantial pure white flower of the early morning changes during the day to a deep pink by sundown. A flower picked in the early morning, and kept in the refrigerator will stay white, but on the evening dinner table it will turn pink during the course of the meal, causing confusion to those not aware of this characteristic, who perhaps wonder whether their alcoholic intake has affected their vision.

Adjacent stands a Pisonia Alba or Grandis, known as the Malayan Lettuce Tree, whose attractive large lemon yellow and pale green leaves I am told are cooked and eaten by the Malays, but I have yet to meet a Malay who claims to have done so. Alongside is an Ixora. Some say that if the Hibiscus is the national flower of Malaysia, then the Ixora should be the flower of South East Asia.

There are about 120 species throughout the tropics, and 20 in Malaysia. Those featuring in gardens are normally from the Indian Ixora group (Ixora Coccinea) which like the full sunlight or from the Javanese Ixora group (Ixora Javanica) which prefer a lightly shaded position. However Corner comments "It is not always easy to distinguish the species, particularly those with orange-red flowers, because they are most variable; the genus appears to be one which is in the process of evolution so that the limits of the species are ill-defined and may be blurred even more by hybridisation with its consequent intermediate forms. Thus there has been both confusion and superfluity in the botanical names". Here we have a pink variety which when purchased featured on the invoice as "Ixora deluxe pink", a name not found in Corner, but elsewhere at 259 Ixoras come in the "orange-red confusion" category.

Here is also a small leafed wiry umbrella like bush which produces numerous magnificently scented tiny white flowers two or three times a year. I suspect it has a vernacular name. All the experts call it Wrightia Religiosa, but the only reference book that I know that confirms this is Francis Ng's "The Tropical Garden City".

Going on to the second clump there is another Acalypha this time a Wilkesiana or the Beefsteak plant which is said to come from Fiji. Corner is not strong on Acalyphas; MacMillan a little more so. Close by stands a Caryota or Fishtail Palm, but more about Palms later. And now a powerful growth of Clerodendron Macrosiphon. Holttum gives us the names of nine different types of Clerodendron growing in Malaysia and we have three at 259. Macrosiphon, or Witches Tongue, so named because of the long purple stamens protruding from tubular white flowers, covers itself with blossom every two or three months, which come out to provide a magnificent display of an evening all to be finished and on the ground by dawn the next day.

Just ten yards further back, enjoying the shade, and filling a gap in the Bamboo curtain which keeps Sayfol School at bay flourishes a recently planted Clerodendron Fragrans or Chinese. This produces a fine white flower smelling powerfully of acid drops. Corner says that Malay people attribute magical properties to many species of Clerodendron and that their Malay names indicate powers to summon spirits. Once again it

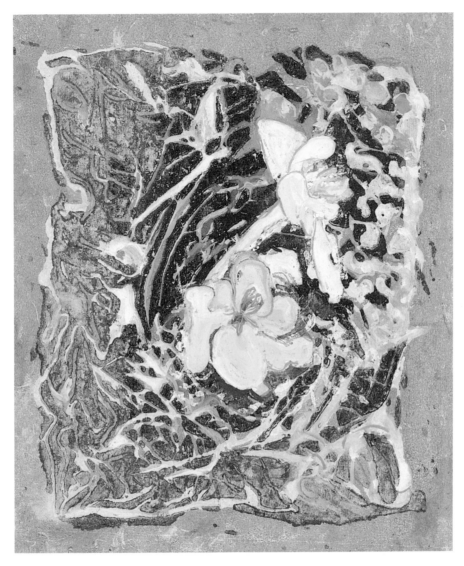

Gardenia Tubifera

seems that I meet the wrong Malays. I have yet to learn what those magical properties are, and whether they exist in the three species at 259.

Now we have a Schefflera Actinophylla, or Australian Ivy-palm, the seedlings of which we are told often begin as epiphytes on the trunks of trees. This is also known as the Umbrella or Octopus Tree. The species is named after J.C. Scheffler, another 17th Century German botanist - one wonders whether 17th Century Germans did anything other than study botany or compose music. Corner tells us there are 400 species of Schefflera; who apart from Mr Corner and Mr Scheffler has counted them?

Alongside is an Ardisia Eliptica, the Sea-Shore Ardisia, which will grow to about 25 feet, assuming it can stand being about 30 miles from the nearest sea-shore. The Malays call it Mata Pelandok, Ayam or Itek depending upon whether its little black berries, which are edible, appear to the beholder more like the eyes of a mouse deer, hen or duck. Finally to complete this clump, we have a newly planted creeper Bauhinia Kockiana, which when we give it something to creep up will eventually provide magnificent clusters of orange flowers. The species, one of 600, is named after the 16th Century French herbalist brothers Jean and Gaspard Bauhin.

### To the South and East

Now back to the pool, and looking south between the pool and the garage there exists an impenetrable bank of Rangoon Creeper (Quisqualis Indica) also known as Drunken Sailor. This is another ferocious grower that has to be cut right back every year or so. About twice a year it covers itself with flowers that start off white and turn crimson, and at dawn and dusk envelope the area with a powerful scent of vanilla.

As the Qursqualis bank moves eastward it merges into another Acalypha, and then a Pseuderanthemum Atropurpureum and then another Polyscias, this one solely distinguished for the fact that inextricably set amongst its root is a Sea Egg or Powder Puff (Haemanthus Multiflorus). This type of lily, of African origin, is fairly unusual and every now and again produces a dramatic flower resembling a 4 inch diameter pink powder puff. I am going to make an effort to separate the bulb sections and see how they perform in pots.

Neighbouring is an infant China Star Jasmine, Tabernaemontana Corymbosa, not in fact a Jasmine, but a type of Periwinkle with small white five pointed star-like flowers, but no Jasmine scent. In Borneo this is known as the Pinwheel Flower, because of its angled star points. Close by there is a Jatropha Pandurifolia, an ancient creature with attractive small red flowers which may well not be with us much longer. One of the three Jatrophas common in Malaysia, I wish mine looked as good as those flourishing by the Changi Airport road in Singapore.

Then we have a Malvaviscus Arboreus Mexicanus known as the Sleeping Hibiscus or Turk's Cap. Continually in bloom its scarlet flowers never fully open. The books say this is not from the Hibiscus family, although to the layman it looks very similar to all the other Hibiscus at 259.

To complete the circuit stands a Duranta Repens, recently Corner tells us renamed Duranta Erecta. The species introduced from America is named after Castor Durantes, the 16th Century Italian herbalist. This rather untidy shrub is probably more attractive to butterflies and moths than to human beings. Certainly there are usually numerous butterflies decorating its branches, and in the evening two or three Humming Bird Hawk Moths can often be seen industriously removing nectar from the small blue flowers with which it is covered. Because of its attractive golden berries, slightly poisonous, it is also known as Golden Dew Drop.

So much for the pool area; I have completed my quarter mile, and it is time to consider seriously the task of getting to the office.

Duranta Repens

# THE AMERICAN QUARTER

# 8

The American Quarter of the garden is bounded by the pool area to the east, a tarmac drive from the entrance gate to the south, the lorong to the west, and separated from the Asia Foundation to the north by a substantial bamboo hedge (a mixture of Bambusa Glaucescens and Bambusa Variegata). This Subbiah clips regularly to keep it to a maximum 8 foot high and hopefully to increase its substantiality.

Leaving for the office after breakfast, my car will have been parked under a 20 foot Bottle Brush tree (Callistemon Lanceolatus or Citrinus), the biggest in Kuala Lumpur says Dato' Mustapha Mahmud, but does he really know? Indigenous to Australia, this is a tree-like shrub with blue green leaves and attractive crimson "bottle brush" flowers 3 or 4 times a year.

Our Bottle Brush is also distinguished in that it is providing succour to a number of clusters of Pigeon Orchid (Dendrobium Crumenatum). These orchids are often found growing on trees in the jungle and in gardens, and are in my view particularly attractive with their un-orchidlike simplicity. The little white flowers, rather like snowdrops, come out 9 or 10 days after a sudden drop in temperature, but only last for 2 days. Unlike most orchids they are powerfully fragrant. This Bottle Brush is also

614    The Turong, or Pigeon Orchid in Borneo
       "... comes into blossom simultaneously on all plants every 9 weeks ..."

57

providing a base for a splendid Asplenium Nidus, said to be one of the oldest epiphytes in the world. Resembling a massive bird's nest (Nidus) it is not difficult to imagine some prehistoric bird brooding in its midst. There is also a thriving Vanilla Fragrans Orchid on this tree, surprising as it prefers a higher altitude. This orchid comes from Mexico and we're told the Aztecs used its essence for flavouring food.

Most of the American Quarter comprises lawn, which as is usual in Malaysia is made up of Cow Grass (Axonopus Compressus). In Britain probably the last thing you want in your lawn is anything like Cow Grass, which resembles the type of plantain that British gardeners look upon as a sign of defeat. But in Malaysia where we are not so fussy about the quality of our lawns, Cow Grass does a good job, grows very fast, and the more you cut it the better it looks, especially if it is treated with a little compost mix once a year, say one-third compost, one-third top soil, one-third sand.

Most Malaysians do not insist on billiard table smoothness for their lawns, and as a result the most commonly used lawn mower is the push type 2-stroke motorised rotary cutter. These are tough animals that don't worry too much if the blade strikes earth, stones, tree roots etc. Replacement blades cost little. Gardeners usually come equipped with their own mowers. We bought one recently when it appeared that Subbiah was spending more time struggling to make his mower work than he spent on cutting our grass. We bought a MASPORT, made in New Zealand, for which in 1988 I paid RM 965.00. It has been a splendid machine, needs an oil change every 3 months, an insignificant amount of petrol, approximately 2 litres for all the grass once a week, although the lawns probably need more frequent attention during rainy periods, and less in times of "drought".

Leaving for the office, looking back over my right shoulder I can see

Tonkin Creeper - Telosma Cordata

the 7 or 8 major trees either within or just inside the bamboo hedge.

First an amalgam of a Durian tree and a jungle tree brand unknown. So much has been written about the Malaysian Durian that I can be brief. The genus name "Durio" comes from the Malay word Durian, which in turn comes from the Malay "duri" meaning a thorn. Large numbers of these cover the hard skin of the fruit, which is about the size of a round or oval coconut. There are 28 different species found in South East Asia, and 13 in Malaysia. In Malaysia the durian has achieved the status of a major cult fruit. The conventional wisdom is that you either love it or hate it. If you hate it, it is probably because of its distinctive, some would say excessively disgusting smell. If you love it, it is for the taste of its creamy fruit.

I am probably the exception. I don't mind the smell, I consider the fruit tastes like a reasonable custard, and I can comfortably live without it.

They do say you should not drink alcohol with Durian, and I know that my wife had trouble combining a glass of gin with the fruit; but in her case it was one glass of gin and about ten durians, and I therefore blame the durian and not the gin.

I am also not sure whether the fruit's reputation as an aphrodisiac is proved; I suspect that smallholders, who grow most of the durians that are for sale, promote this quality as a marketing device.

My Durian tree once produced six durians, but the squirrels got the lot. As well as being swamped by its next door neighbour, it provides support for a massive climbing Scindapsus Pictus (the Money Plant), and it also suffered the loss of its top 15 foot in a major Sumatra in early 1991 (The Money Plant survived well, and I take this as an extremely good omen).

Adjacent is an Australian product, a 60-foot Moreton Bay or Hoop Pine, Araucaria Cunninghamii, named after the Australian Cunningham brothers botanists in the 19th Century. This is a distinctive tree with its whorls of foliage which unfortunately tend to fall off in barrow loads in heavy winds, but which when they are not doing so provide accomodation for a large community of bats. In Australia this can grow to two hundred feet. A passion flower creeper, Passiflora Coccinea, is wrapping itself around this tree to a height of about 20 feet. Its startling red blossoms are magnificent, but I hope it will not stifle the tree.

Beside it is a Royal Palm (Roystonea Regia) but more about palms when we reach the French Quarter in the next Chapter. Then we have a small group of shrubs comprising a Golden Hibiscus, and a Congea Tomentosa, a native of Burma, and sometimes called a "Shower Orchid". This is a new arrival, a creeper that hopefully will be covered with small white flowers and lilac coloured bracts.

Alongside is a rather similar creature, a Petrea Volubilis, from Central America. This has become far too voluble since being cut back, and has ceased to produce its attractive lilac flowers in protest. It houses the only snake which we believe we have in the garden, an attractive multi-coloured Paradise Tree Snake - only mildly venomous to human beings. This is also known as the "Sandpaper Vine" for reasons which become clear if you stroke its leaves. Also in this cluster exists a Stenolobium or Tecoma Stans (Yellow Bells, self-explanatory) which performs magnificently provided it receives no compost, no fertilisers and no attention of any sort.

Here is also a mango tree which has failed to produce a mango and which also had a rough time in the 1991 Sumatra. It is now cut back and used as a support for a recently installed Pandorea Jasminoides creeper, the Bower Plant of Queensland.

And last is the famous Tanjong Tree (Mimusops Elengi) well known for its curled leaves and highly scented little white flowers, and a feature of every kampong in the Peninsula.

This brings us into the jungle corner presided over by two 50 foot trees, a scruffy Mexican Lilac (Gliricidia Sepium); not just ours, they are always scruffy, but they do have attractive lilac type flowers, which make up for their habit of shedding small branches at regular intervals. Next door to it stands one of the features of the garden, a well established magnificent Lithocarpus - at least John Wyatt Smith, a former head of the Forest Research Institute of Malaysia, pronounced it so; i.e. one of the 10 or so oak family to grow in Malaysia, although this one has yet to produce an acorn. It makes up for it with its thick foliage and gnarled trunk, and asks to be photographed by day and flood-lit by night. Some claim this is the oldest tree in a garden in Kuala Lumpur.

STEPHANOTIS FLORIBUNDA

Stephanotis Floribunda

Deployed around the base of these and enjoying the shade are two Ixoras, Javanica and Sinensis, and a Randia Macrantha which produces a dramatic display of primrose coloured "Angels Trumpets" 2 or 3 times a year.

Also in this shade area is an attractive little tree, now about 15 foot high, a Cordia Subcordata (named after yet another 16th Century German botanist V. Cordus), locally called the "Sea Trumpet". Common on the sandy coasts of the Indian and West Pacific oceans and particularly so on the North West Coast of Peninsular Malaysia, it will I am told grow to 50 foot, and is attractive with its little trumpet shaped orange flowers. Just beside it is a powerful growth of Lobster Claw (Heliconia Humilis), common in every garden and obviously named. Also enjoying the shade and up against the west border hedge of Chinese Privet (Ligustrum Sinense) is a small grove of Rhapis Palm (Rhapis Excelsa). Rhapis leaves are widely used in Indian temples, and for a period we regularly had a visitor who considered himself responsible for maintaining temple stock levels. He would enter through a hole in the fence; our dogs would bark courageously from a safe distance; our visitor undeterred would proceed with his harvesting. Fortunately he was more frightened of human beings, and when eventually my daughter Tamsin confronted him, he left at speed never to return.

We have reached the gate, we turn right into the lorong and proceed to the office.

Rhapis Palm

# THE FRENCH QUARTER

# 9

I usually return to 259 shortly before sunset, which is a good time. All gardens look better at dawn and dusk; at dawn because of that special light and because of the aura of freshness; at dusk because the failing light hides those imperfections in the garden that we have tried to ignore during the day. And dusk, which often follows rain, brings with it a welcome coolness after the tropical heat of the day.

Another point favouring these times is that most flowering trees and shrubs are at their most fragrant. Fragrance has been the prime qualification for getting planted at 259, attractive flowering the second, and rarity the third.

Arriving at the gate of 259, the first major attraction is a magnificent White Chempaka tree (Michelia Alba). As mentioned before Chempaka is a Hindu word used for a number of trees in Asia which have white or yellow fragrant flowers. The flowers of the White and Orange Chempaka are often sold in Muslim markets or shops for decorating the hair or being made into garlands. There are 45 species of Michelia, and these are from the Magnolia genus. The White Chempaka comes from China, and is reasonably common in Peninsular Malaysia, although I have been told that ours is the biggest one in Kuala Lumpur.

---

300   **Indian Coral Trees**

"Erythrina Indica is often mentioned by poets - since Krishna stole it from the Celestial Garden for his wives, it has been under a curse, and is never used in Hindu worship. In Malabar, it provides a support for Betel Pepper, it is often used for hedges... its leaves and bark are used medicinally"

This is particularly satisfactory as it was given to us in a pot about 1 foot high in 1976 by Jim Champion, who was then representing the RTZ interests in Malaysia, and more important was at the time my Chairman.

One of the reasons why Jim Champion was good on trees and shrubs was that his father, Sir Harry Champion, was the most senior forestry official in India before becoming Professor of Forestry at Oxford. Jim, his father, and his son David, were in turn scholars of New College, Oxford, and would surely have created a record had they all been present at the same gaudy in 1983; sadly not to be owing to Sir Harry's sudden death a few days before the event.

In 1977 Jim was responsible for giving my wife a copy of Professor H F Chin's excellent "Malaysia Flowers in Colour", essential reading for the RIB and in fact for anyone interested in stocking a garden in Malaysia.

Strangely, the White Chempaka does not feature in Professor Chin's book. Ours is now 21 years old, and has grown to approximately 70 foot. It produces its cream coloured flowers 4 or 5 times a year which soak the area in fragrance; altogether a very special tree. Special incidentally also to Silver Leaf monkeys who seem to enjoy eating Chempaka leaves, and every now and again make an invasion.

The French Quarter essentially comprises a lawn, in the middle of which stands our Chempaka, and which is edged on the "Club Med" side by four groups of trees.

Firstly, standing sentinel to the right of the gate post, a pair to the Mexican Lilac across the drive, is a Caribbean Pine (Pinus Caribaea). A native of the West Indies, this was probably the first tree Christopher Columbus set eyes on when discovering the West Indies on that epic voyage in the Santa Maria from Barcelona in 1492, backed by Queen Isabella of Spain.

Decorating its 50 foot trunk is a huge Philodendron Creeper,

66

although which of the many South American species this is remains a mystery.

Close by is another Frangipani (Plumeria Accuminata) this time a pink one, and in the shade area provided by these two trees there flourishes a host of jungle creatures, genus recognisable but on the whole species not. A number of Dieffenbachia, immigrants from South and Central America, (the Edes tells us that Herr Dieffenbach was the head gardener at the Austrian Imperial Palace of Schonbrunn in Vienna in the 1830's); a Tree Fern and a Maiden Hair Fern, a clump of Dracaena Surculosa (which most people think is a type of bamboo); a Pandanus (pineapple family), a Brunfelsia Americana known in the West Indies as "Lady of the Night" whose fragrant flowers initially white turn to primrose yellow, a Pseuderanthemum Reticulatum, another Exocaria, and more Lobster Claws and Polyscias. Amongst these are a number of Clerodendron Paniculata, the Pagoda plant, and reigning supreme in this area when in flower are clusters of Crinum Giganteum, a heavily scented large white flower also known as the Java Lily. Bordering the area is a fringe of Wedelia Trilobata ground cover that flourishes in the shade with its yellow flowers.

Along the perimeter is a substantial grove of bamboo (Bambusa Vulgaris). Each stem grows up to 40 or 50 feet, and 4 or 5 inches in diameter, starting off green and turning to gold. In the growing season, there are reports of shoots growing 6 inches a day; but 2 inches is the best I have measured. At the foot of these bamboos, a mass of Heliconia Psittacorum Lathispatha and Rubra do quite well, and two young Birds of Paradise, Strelitzia Reginae. These are native to South Africa, and claim to be named after George III's wife whose family name was Mechlenburgh-Strelitz and who was a patron of botany. Moving further round the perimeter we come to an area principally occupied by members of the palm family. There are many hundreds of different palms in the world, and many of them seem to go under different names in different places. Certainly some of our local names don't tie up with the references in other countries.

Holttum (Gardening in the Lowlands of Malaya), only reserves 6 pages for palms and these include a mere 10 varieties. Amongst ours are the well-known Royal Palm, (Roystonae Regia) which looks appropriately regal, two Fan Palms (Livistona Rotundifolia), a Sealing-Wax Palm or Pinang Rajah (Cyrtostachys Lakka) truly dramatic with its red sealing wax coloured stems, and a "Triangular" Palm, so called because of the shape of its trunk.

While on the subject of palms I should mention the Australian Ptychosperma which flourishes at the base of the Lithocarpus near the entrance gate. Elsewhere in the Russian quarter we also have a splendid clump of Chrysalidocarpus from Madagascar, attractive with its yellow stems and golden leaves. Dotted round the garden there are numerous Fishtail Palms (Caryota) numerous because of the thousands of seeds which they regularly scatter. We don't have the fan shaped Travellers' Palm (Ravenala Madagascariensis), possibly Malaysia's most well known palm, although it too comes from Madagascar and is strictly not a palm but from the banana family. (In Indonesia it is known as Pisang Kipas, the Banana Fan). Some say it is called the Travellers' Palm because its cup-shaped leaf bases hold drinking water for thirsty travellers; others because self-seeded it aligns itself facing east. We did have an elderly example of the ubiquitous Coconut Palm (Cocos Nucifera) which we had to deal with before it is dealt with us - falling timber or coconuts; now we have one of its progeny about 6 foot high. If we find an African Oil Palm (Elaeis Guineensis) or better known in Malaysia simply as Oil Palm, it gets rooted out quickly. Featuring in plantations which cover much of Malaysia it is a generator of a significant percentage of the country's wealth. We do not want it in the garden as it takes up much space, and its fruit attract rats in

68

quantities.

Going back to our Palm area, there is more Rhapis Excelsa which we have described earlier. There is also a Pleomele Reflexa; although not a palm, to the RIB it looks like one and merges well with its neighbours. Similarly the Umbrella Grass (Cyperus Involucratus) which thrives in the wet looks sufficiently palm like. This is a cousin of Cyperus Papyrus from which the English word "paper" is derived, the original Egyptian "Papyrus" being formed from the tissues of the stem.

So much for palms. Now for the next item on the perimeter, and a major casualty of the 1991 Sumatra, a very substantial Malayan Banyan Tree (Ficus Microcarpa). Yes, Ficus is a fig tree, but not the sort of fig tree that we normally think of. There are about 1,000 species of Ficus, and about 100 in Malaysia alone. There are no fancy fruit on the Malayan Banyan. It is however a dramatic tree with its aerial roots like brown string or tassels hanging from the branches sometimes down to ground level. This is similar to but not to be confused with the Indian Banyan Tree, from under which justice is traditionally dispensed, although a few of these do exist in Malaysia.

We have planted a Flame of the Forest (Delonix Regia) to fill the gap left by the Ficus. Every mature garden used to have one of these. The orange "umbrella" of a Delonix in blossom is an essential component. Other areas of the gap have been taken over by a dark blue Morning Glory, Ipomoea Learii; magnificent until noon by which time on all but the coolest days its flowers will have withered away.

One more feature decorates the French Quarter, a small mound probably the site of a major tree no longer with us. Here is another prolific Clerodendron Fragrans (Chinense) partially shaded by another well known Malaysian tree, the Rose of India or the Queen's Flower, or the Malay Bungor, (Lagerstroemia Speciosa named after M Lagerstroem, an

18th Century Swedish patron of science). This should grow to about 40 foot and we are still waiting for its magnificent pink flowers.

In the semi-shade of the infant "Bungor", we have 5 Hibiscus including a Coral Hibiscus (Hibiscus Schizopetalus), another Rose of Sharon (Hibiscus Mutabilis) and 3 colourful varieties of Hibiscus Rosa-Sinensis. Also in this grouping is a Thunbergia Affinis which has for a number of years shown much promise but little performance in producing deep violet trumpet-shaped flowers with a yellow throat. Our patience with this one is running out. Just adjacent is a hugely flourishing Tabernaemontana, so similar to the Gardenia Jasminoides (Cape Jasmine) except that the attractive white flowers have no fragrance. Overshadowing this is a very ancient Indian Laburnum (Cassia Fistula) which once a year presents a staggering sight with its pendulous groups of golden yellow flowers.

Now a few words about dogs, as there was always a little bit of competition between our dogs and those in the French accommodation next door. Anyone who is fortunate enough to have an acre of garden will find it a good excuse to own 2 or 3 dogs, and during our time in Malaysia, we have always been lucky in this way. We have never gone for the smart breeds, and instead have trusted in the pye dog, which the Oxford dictionary describes as the "Ownerless Mongrel of the East". This animal is normally about the size of a large spaniel, has a short white or sandy coat, and a pointed nose, pointed ears and a curly tail. Given a little attention it is the brightest and most faithful animal you can find anywhere. We have always relied on the SPCA for our supply. For years the SPCA has been run by Max and Mea Wheatley. Max served with the Australian army in North Africa in World War II, and since then has lived in the country, where in earlier days he was a famous figure both on the cricket and the polo field. But what magnificent work they have done at the SPCA. Kuala Lumpur

Garlic Vine - Pseudocalymma Alliaceum

does not have a great reputation for looking after animals, and there are accordingly an awful lot of horror stories.

The SPCA does a grand job in alleviating the misery of many of these animals and at the same time providing people like us with a number of life-long friends. I will only mention four. Our first was a white pye dog called Booty. Amongst the many things we remember him for was sticking with our small son Mark then aged two, when he decided to go for a walk in the jungle unaccompanied by his parents or his amah. Both he and Booty were looking very relaxed when they were found. Then there was Piglet, half Alsatian and half pye, so called because of her AA Milne appearance when collected as a very small puppy form the SPCA. She lived for 17 years, a truly remarkable age for a Malaysian dog, but even her old bones, buried under the mango tree, fail to produce any mangoes. Thirdly I must mention Bramble (although not an SPCA product), who also lived for 17 years, if for no other reason than that she was a virgin birth - or seemed to be so at the time.

I spoke of Jim Champion earlier, but I didn't mention two other things for which he was famous. Firstly, was his lack of interest in motor cars. This was incomprehensible to his Australian head office, where executives spend much of their working hours checking up on the size of and accessories on their colleagues' company supplied vehicles. Has it got sports tyres? Fog lights? Alloy wheels? A sun roof? etc. etc.

Jim on being asked by his solicitous chairman what sort of car he would like replied that he didn't really mind, but that he'd prefer a blue one. Melbourne never quite recovered from this. Jim was also famous for his dog Shady, a golden Labrador who used to travel everywhere with him in his blue car. Shady was aristocratic, probably pre-Norman Conquest. She loved two things, first of all travelling in Jim's car, and secondly watching television. For this purpose, she had a special sofa in the

Champion's library in their house just off Jalan U Thant.

Because of Shady's impeccable lineage, it had never been possible to find for her a husband who was sufficiently grand. It was therefore a very considerable shock to quite a number of people, Shady included, when in the course of quite an interesting television programme, Shady suddenly produced a small black puppy, followed in the course of the night, by three more.

My daughter Tamsin had always been promised the pick of the litter should Shady ever have puppies, and curiously picked Bramble, who was the most miserable looking of the lot. But Bramble confused us all, grew into a magnificent lady quite worthy of her distinguished and beautiful mother. But who was the father? Nobody knows, but we have our suspicions. At the time Jim had an Australian assistant who had a very powerful male Weimarana. Apart from her Labrador looks, Bramble has some strong Weimarana characteristics, and I have a notion that a certain Weimarana at one stage must have deceived the chaperon. All I can say is that a Weimarana/Labrador mishap was an excellent animal to have about the place.

Fudgie, half pye and half boxer, is still with us. Fudgie is awe-inspiringly fierce in aspect, and so has some value from the point of view of the insurance company. But Fudgie is not courageous, and can be guaranteed to be either asleep or at the other end of the garden if ever an unwelcome visitor draws near.

So much for dogs, and for that matter so much for the French Quarter.

8m Umbrella Grass

# THE RUSSIAN WALL

# 10

Come the weekend an element of my time revolves around the Russian Wall. At the north end of the wall there is space for storing piles of bonfire ash, the four bays of maturing compost, and a supply of sharp sand. Further south up against the wall there is a long inelegant timber structure used for the storage of garden equipment and also a secondary studio for my wife's sculpting activities. From the Russian compound two large African Tulip trees (Spathodea Campanulata) regularly used to shed branches on to its asbestos roof, which the Embassy used to have promptly repaired, sometimes even before the arrival of my irritable letters of complaint.

In the days following Glasnost when one imagines funds for running the embassy were scarce, quite often junior diplomats were despatched with large axes to repair the damage; and on one occasion when some windows had been broken by some small boys at the embassy, my wife swears that the ambassador himself appeared in dark glasses leading the wretched father who was grasping some putty and a sheet of 4mm glass.

The February 1991 Sumatra removed everything removable from these two Tulip trees so it will be some time until we are bothered again.

Their orange red flowers are more attractive than their generic habit of dropping branches and often collapsing altogether owing to their quick growth and their roots which grow laterally rather than downward.

To the south the wall continues, but the 259 garden ends with a Cassia Multijuga, attractive with its candlestick style clusters of yellow flowers, and another Lettuce Tree. Partially camouflaging the shed is a row of Papaya trees (Carica Papaya), sold to us as an "Exotica" hybrid.

Papayas grow quickly and the females of the right varieties produce excellent fruit frequently provided regularly composted. In Scotland you start the day with porridge; in Malaysia with a slice of papaya. With some lime squeezed over it, preferably half a Musk Lime (Limau Kesturi), about 1 inch in diameter and internally orange rather than the usual lime green, papaya makes an excellent porridge alternative.

The Papaya row ends with a Gardenia Tubifera, the species named after the 18th Century American naturalist, A Garden. The Tubifera, or Water Gardenia, can grow to 60 foot, and produces splendid flowers which start cream white and fall on the third day when they have become deep orange. A space next door is reserved for a Kedah Gardenia (Gardenia Carinata) which has magnificent yellow flowers, and should grow to about 40 foot; these are both natives of Malaysia. Elsewhere we have the more common White Gardenia, or Cape Jasmin (Gardenia Jasminoides), a native of China with its frequent highly scented white flowers.

This area lies to the east of the quarters occupied over the years by household staff. Peter Verity, one of our regular visitors from London, has suggested that my next essay into literature should be a Soap Opera including items from the unending dramas that the servant's quarters at 259 seem to generate.

In the 1970's Ah Ming, our old Hainanese cook boy, used to entertain the children by dancing ridiculous jigs in between producing the fried eggs for breakfast. Ah Moy, an amah who followed him, brought her very ancient father to spend his last days in peace and quietness with her, and then laid him out in all his finery for the funeral, burning enough paper money the while to keep him in luxury for at least a million years. Ramai, who followed Ah Moy, was over-enthusiastic with the religious candles, and burnt the quarters down. I well remember the laconic voice on the telephone of Keith Mayn, a New Zealand colleague who was house-sitting with his wife Catherine while we were in London - "The bad news is that there has been a major fire. The good news is that the wind changed, and only the quarters have been lost". The brunt of the losses were indeed from my wife's studio and included many of her earlier drawings and sketches. Her studio in itself would provide material for my Soap Opera, but I would be standing on dangerous ground if I were to include the numerous personalities who have been there to get their or their children's portraits done.

More recently, Ramai's successor Saroja died in sad circumstance leaving two orphaned children. The 6-hour Hindu ritual to ensure that she rests in peace involved the burning of uncounted boxes of spices, fruit, oils and scented wood, and much incantation.

Moving on there is a clump of Scarlet Canna (Canna Orientalis). These South American imports also come in pink and yellow, and like bagpipes are best admired from a considerable distance. Nearby, there is a self-seeded Durian tree about which we have already said quite enough, some Caryota Palms, and two substantial clumps of Torch Ginger (Phaeomeria Speciosa) locally known as Kantan.

Kantan comes from Mauritius and its palm-like leaves grow to 15 foot, shading its large waxy pink flowers, that is if they reach that stage since as buds they are much used in curries, and particularly in the famous

Kenanga or Ylang-Ylang - Cananga Odorata

Penang Laksa. Alongside is our Christmas tree of a number of years, now put out to grass, a pine tree to date unnamed.

Neighbouring there is a mass of Pandan (Pandanus Amaryllifolius); its pineapple type leaves also used in Malay cooking have a heavy musky scent, similar to that of a Civet cat. Further in from the wall there is another Polyscias, and a group comprising Frangipani, this time a yellow Accuminata, a Pong-Pong Tree (Cerbera Odollam) and a cluster of Banana plants. The Pong-Pong Tree recently became a great favourite with the

Kuala Lumpur and Singapore civic authorities for roadside planting, but is now going out of fashion owing to its massive capacity for dropping leaves, and because its fruit which look like green oranges are a bit poisonous. Some say its latex is also blinding and for this reason, like Exocaria, the tree is sometimes also known by Malays as Buta Buta; probably not the best type of roadside decoration, but attractive and its little white flowers smell like Primroses in the early morning. Given regular compost the Bananas are developing well. These are Pisang Mas, "one of the finest East Asian edible bananas, the flesh being rich yellow and very sweet" according to MacMillan. Ours comply well with this definition.

Adjacent and concealing an unsightly slotted-angle climbing frame is another of my favourites, a Tonkin Creeper (Telosma Cordata). The flowers, much like upside down Cowslips, are concealed beneath the profuse foliage. But you are not in doubt when the Tonkin creeper is in bloom as its honey-sweet scent is quite overpowering.

Nearby are examples of a truly indigenous Malaysian tree, two splendid young Tembusu. The Tembusu (Fagraea Fragrans) named after J T Fagraeus, an 18th Century Swedish naturalist, will grow to 100 foot and will eventually cover itself with sweet smelling white blossom once a year. The Tembusu is a slow grower and enjoys ill-drained laterite soil, and does not react well to applications of my compost. In fact in its early days it contracted a "virus" as a result of which its leaves curled up, and according to our expert these had to be removed and burnt sharply.

Marking the junction of the wall and the bamboo hedge stands another Tanjong Tree, and 15 yards down the hedge grows one of the rarer trees in Malaysia. This is a Maingaya Malayana, from the Witch-Hazel family (Hamamelis). The story is that one tree was discovered in the 19th Century on Penang Hill by Dr A C Maingay, the then medical officer of the Malacca Prison. His official duties were clearly not over taxing, as Dr

Maingay found the time to develop into a distinguished botanist in his short life of 33 years. The seeds of his one Maingaya Malayana were collected and planted in various sites down the Peninsula and the tree is still rare. Ours came from Henry Barlow, and as the supplier of a number of our more special plants, he merits at least a paragraph here.

The substantial Barlow rubber and palm oil plantations were transferred to the Government in the course of the Malaysianisation activities of the 1970's and 80's. Henry Barlow in the meantime had bought the Genting Sempah tea estate, which lies about 2,000 feet above sea level on the way up to the Genting Highlands development. The estate was first planted in the 1920's by Choo Kia Peng, a scion of one of the founding families of Kuala Lumpur, principally to produce not tea, but tea seeds for the industry. Established at Genting Sempah, Henry Barlow concentrates on growing things more for pleasure than profit. He is an international authority on moths, and has written and edited numerous books, including H F MacMillan's "Tropical Planting and Gardening" (edited together with Messrs. I Enoch and R A Russell). He also carries out the honorary tasks of being Treasurer to the Malaysian Nature Society and Secretary to the Malaysian Heritage Trust, and was recently Chairman of the British Malaysia Industry and Trade Association.

Before we move in from the Russian Wall, a paragraph is also required on birds. One of the results of the enlarged tree and shrub count at 259 is the most satisfactory increase in the bird population. As the roar of the Jalan Ampang traffic increases in volume daily, and as trees and shrubs elsewhere in the city disappear under the remorseless avalanche of condominium construction, so does the bird population at 259 multiply.

The dawn chorus is impressive and the permanent or transient population of birds reads like the index to M W F Tweedie's "Common Malay Birds". There are usually two or three pairs of Yellow Vented Bulbuls, in

Chalice Vine - Solandra Nitida

the first half of the year industriously building nests in ridiculously accessible places; Magpie or Straits Robins which sing like a blackbird during the day, particularly just after the rain, and quite often during the night as well are always in evidence. You can always spot two or three pairs of Mynahs talking incessantly and stalking about on the grass with an air of great self-assurance, where their alertness preserves them from the too approximate attentions of cats and dogs.

Gangs of four or five Black-naped Orioles are frequent visitors in the tree tops where they can be spotted more from their bell-like calls than from their dramatic yellow plumage which provides such good camouflage. I usually disturb a White-breasted Kingfisher when I go for my early morning swim; he then sits on a nearby tree watching me balefully until I leave to enable him to complete his ablutions. Since we got rid of the last of our ancient coconut trees, we have not seen so much of the Golden-backed Woodpeckers which regularly used to feed off them. With his scarlet crest, black and white face and golden back, this is one of Malaysia's most magnificent birds.

Often we get visited by a pack of Glossy Tree Starlings, small bottle green birds with scarlet eyes. We occasionally hear but rarely see the tiny Long-tailed Tailor Bird, so small that it is normally only evident from the movement of the leaves in a shrub, and from its quite excruciatingly tedious call. More often recently we see the Common Koel. Black with scarlet eyes and about the size of a crow with a long tail, it flops about in the trees and advertises its presence with an excessively loud and frequently repeated call. There is usually a pair of Barred Ground Doves, strutting around on the ground, and very tame. In the summer months there is generally a Blue-throated Bee-eater to be seen catching insects before rain. It is replaced in the winter, but more occasionally, by the similar Brown-breasted Bee-eater. At the foot of the French Quarter hedge, particularly in

82

the rainy season, there can often be seen a White-Breasted Water Hen (Ruak-Ruak) walking on its long legs, making its "ruak ruak" call whence it gets its Malay name.

At night of course as everywhere in Peninsular Malaysia we frequently hear and sometimes see the Long-tailed Nightjar generally known as the Tock-Tock Bird. Its bursts of two, three or four "tocks" in the early evening increase to up to a hundred before dawn, most unattractive to these who are not air-conditioned and who find difficulty sleeping.

Finally, four rare but notable visitors. The first is a Serpent Eagle, which lives off snakes but I am told finds chickens easier and less dangerous to catch. Another rare visitor is a Lemon Crested Cockatoo which has clearly escaped from captivity and done a little breeding. On one occasion 4 were seen circling the area, shrieking in their own inimitable fashion as if each call were their last.

Then recently a Lesser Blue-winged Pitta was seen lurking in the undergrowth near the pool, like a small plump Kingfisher, but with even more brilliant red, white, black, buff, green and blue colouring. And equally surprisingly, we were recently visited in the dining room by a Japanese Sparrow Hawk in hot pursuit of a Starling. The Starling then took temporary refuge in the kitchen while the hawk avoided the fan and swung back outside in search of other prey.

So much for the bird population of 259 Jalan Ampang; not bad for the centre of a major city.

Pitta

# ROUND THE HOUSE

# II

259 is not a grand establishment and it does not take a long time to walk around the house. We can deal with the area under three headings, firstly the north side, secondly the terrace area on the south side, and thirdly the "fragrant garden" to the east. The perimeter of the house is covered by the usual 5 foot roof overhang, and this area provides an ideal place for displaying potted plants; not your usual 1 foot high hole-in-the bottom common job, but the 3 foot high Chinese egg-pot type, a glazed pot in which the Chinese still store and transport preserved eggs. These became particularly popular for garden use, and are now made for the purpose. A number of these on the north side are lined up containing Bougainvillea, (Bunga Kertas or the Paper Flower). With composting, Bougainvilleas do excellently in pots frequently colourful with their bracts of various shades ranging from bright purple to red, to pink, to orange, and white. We have a particularly attractive one with red bracts and variegated green/yellow leaves. Holttum tells us that Bougainvilleas should be pruned after flowering and then composted to produce new growth.

Most Bougainvilleas flower after a dry period, and so the general principle for potted Bougainvillea is that feeding and watering should stop once the growth is achieved, when starving and shortage of water

**The Neem**
"... Melia Azadirachta is described by the poets as the type of all that is bitter; and its bark is said to be a fair substitute for Cinchona in cases of fever etc. The leaves are commonly applied to wounds, either fresh or in poultice ..."

encourages flowering. The RIB should experiment.

Amongst the Bougainvilleas there are two or three Adenium Coetanum, common in East Africa and Arabia, (named after Aden) where it is known as the Desert Rose. In Malaysia it grows well in pots to about 3 foot high with thick fleshy twisted branches, and is continuously colourful with vivid crimson trumpet shaped flowers. There are also 3 pots of Keng Hua (Epiphyllum Oxypetalum) which originate not from China as you might imagine, but from Mexico and Brazil. They are from the Cactus family and once or twice a year produce large fragrant white flowers from their fleshy leaves. These come out for one night, starting to unfold at about 8.00 p.m. and being fully open before midnight.

At the end of the row at the north-west corner of the house is a Euphorbia Splendens, from the Cactus family, very prickly with small leaves and very small bright flowers. This comes from Madagascar where it is known as the "Crown of Thorns". Round the corner to the front door car porch area exists a continually changing collection of pots of various Caladiums, Anthuriums, Dracaenas, Dieffenbachias and Ferns. Subbiah considers that this area is his responsibility, and this means daily watering and frequent re-arrangement which confuses us all. Pots continue around the house to the terrace area on the south side, but only for those that can take the sun.

### The Terrace Area

For anyone who considers that breakfast is a serious meal, being able to attack the papaya against a background of tropical vegetation definitely contributes to this important occasion. Anna Plowden has been visiting us from London for some years, originally for jungle forays, and more recently she has been providing me with much advice and guidance on this book. Anna is a truly serious breakfaster and shares my views on this matter. Planted round the little terrace on the French side of 259 are six rather attractive items, over and above the various mobile pots. There are two Frangipani, one an ancient substantial Obtusa, well covered with Pigeon Orchids, and a newly planted Accuminata, put in for its magnificent brick red-orange flowers. In between is an Indian Coral Tree, or Tiger's Claw, Erythrina Orientalis (formerly Indica) and known as Dadap in Malay, which is famous for its long panicles of dark crimson flowers. Ours is doing well and should grow to about 20 feet and provide a pleasant shade. This is a sea shore tree common from India to the Pacific Isles.

To the right of the terrace is some trellis work where two creepers compete. Clearly winning in this competition is a Garlic Vine (Pseudocalymma Alliaceum), a native of Brazil, and common in Kelantan. It covers itself regularly with a mass of purple flowers with a creamy throat, and if you crush the leaves you will know why it is called the Garlic Vine.

Losing the battle next to it is a Madagascar Jasmine, Stephanotis Floribunda. Holttum says this is naturally slow and needs well drained soil and a sunny place. It has yet to produce the beautiful white fragrant wax like flowers for which it is famous, and perhaps would do better on the east side of the house.

To complete the scene on the left is a wall built in a burst of enthusiasm over a weekend visit by Derek Edmondson, an old friend and colleague from Crittall days. Up against this wall is a well established Kemuning or Mock Orange tree, Murraya Paniculata, named after a Scotsman, J A Murray 1740-1791. This is indigenous to Malaysia and rather special. The little flowers, highly fragrant, appear at irregular intervals normally at night, and coincidentally often when we have a dinner party on the terrace. Of all the fragrant flowers at 259, these are undoubtedly the most dramatic and pervasive. When the Kemuning is in blossom everyone in the house knows about it. The wood of the tree is very hard, rather like box wood, and the roots of the tree are pale and much prized for making into handles and sheaths for the Malay Kris. I have seen a gun cupboard made out of Kemuning which alas is not for sale.

Even if you are not the least interested in trees or shrubs, the 259 terrace area provides remarkably good surroundings for the consumption of food and drink. If we'd known how long we were destined to live at 259, we would have kept a record of the times we dined on this terrace. More often than not our dinners coincided with the arrival of an overseas visitor, or the departure of friends at the end of a tour. Such occasions were too infrequent as we never seemed to be able to come near to deleting everyone on our "guilt list". Normally these events were essentially relaxed and as far as I can recall we only came near to bloodshed once. This was when two friends, one Australian (male) and one Pakistani (female) become decidedly over-excited on the subject of Apartheid.

A memorable occasion was when we had a small dinner party for Joan Fenner and her daughter and son-in-law, Susie and Mark Chilton. They were all re-visiting K.L. having lived here for many years. Joan is the widow of Sir Claude Fenner who was Inspector-General of Police (IGP) at Independence.

Tun Haniff Omar, the then IGP, and his wife Toh Puan Hamidah also came along accompanied to our surprise by the official police video film unit. I may be wrong, but on reflection I believe this is the only event during our time in Malaysia which has resulted in our having a police record.

### The East Side

Looking out from my study window eastwards, there is a small lawn about 15 yards by 20 surrounded by the kitchen area on one side and the garage and store area on the other. The garage naturally has cars in it from

Yesterday, Today & Tomorrow - Brunfelsia Pauciflora Floribunda

time to time, but its most famous period was when it was converted into an indoor cricket net in the days before my son Mark decided to concentrate on rather more energetic sports. The grass area gets smaller daily as a massive Acalypha, an Alamanda Cathartica, a Mango tree and an orange flowered Hibiscus compete for space. We have a Chalice Vine taking over the Mango tree, not a concern as its small mangos are fit only for chutney. The Chalice Vine (Solandra Nitida) comes from Mexico and its striking appearance makes up for its lack of a scent.

Six attractive additions have been included to compensate for the lack of fragrance. These are now thriving just outside my study window; another Wrightea Religiosa; a Jasminum Sambac, known as the Arabian Jasmine, which occasionally produces clusters of little white very sweet smelling flowers; and a "Yesterday, Today and Tomorrow" shrub (Brunfelsia Pauciflora Floribunda) which covers itself with a mass of purple flowers yesterday, which change to white today, and fall tomorrow, and are staggeringly fragrant while doing all this.

Next to the Brunfelsia is a little Chempaka Figo, a cousin of our magnificent Michelia Alba. Figo is its Cochin Chinese name, and it is also known as the Dwarf Chempaka, but could not be less like its cousin. It grows into a small dark leaved bush, and has yellow flowers with an intense smell of ripe bananas.

With a very different type of fragrance is a Dwarf Kenanga, native to South East Asia, and sometimes cultivated for its greenish yellow flowers which produce the famous scent known in the Philippines as Ylang-ylang, or in Java as Kenanga, and which is the basis for Chanel No. 5. MacMillan tells us that 200kg of flowers produce 1kg of essence, and that one hectare planted with 370 trees produces 3,350 kg of flowers. Our sixth fragrance producer is another Frangipani, this one recently planted which hopefully will produces deep red flowers.

Two more non-scent producing items complete this area, a Mus-saenda Philippica, with its rose pink sepals, common on every roadside in Kuala Lumpur, and near the kitchen, rare in Kuala Lumpur but common in the north of the Peninsula, a Nim tree, Melia Indica. In India the Nim tree is famous for its valuable medicinal properties, its most famous product being Margosa oil. Almost every part of the tree is medically useful - leaves, bark, white fragrant flowers, and fruit. Certainly when my daughter had chicken pox, the leaves of the Nim tree converted into a paste with rice provided the most soothing result. My Nim tree which was obtained 1 foot high in a pot from Penang, is now 20 foot high and has taken over the area with a seriously adverse effect on the local drainage system.

Wrightea Religiosa

# THE MAGIC

# 12

So that completes a short walk round what some people might say is a rather ordinary garden. But to a gardener no garden is ordinary, no tree is identical, no flower is identical, and anyway no plant is the same today as it was yesterday. And of course anything that you yourself have planted is uniquely special to you.

However small or simple your garden may be, the more involved you get in developing the magic, the more that magic will envelope you and those about you.

In fact we had some proof of this when after a long absence from Malaysia in Europe, on a visit to 259 my eldest daughter Carola became engaged to be married within days of her arrival. And seven days later she was married. The nocturnal mix of Chempaka, Frangipani and Kenanga makes powerful magic indeed.

Barred Ground Dove

"The highly scented petals of Cananga Odorata are much loved by the native ladies of the Malay islands. They are used in the manufacture of Florida Water, and of the llang-llang of the Philippine islands"

700    **Foliage & Fruit of the Tamarind and Flowers & Fruit of the Papaw in Java**
"… Carica Papaya likewise possesses the rare and remarkable property of making fresh meat tender in a few hours …"

94

# Reference Guide

The following information is culled from my personal experience or perceptions. I hasten to state that many items may lack academic or botanical accuracy - the potential Ph.D. should be cautious. Caveat emptor.

C    Controllable creeper
C+   Rampant creeper
F    Fruit

CHAPTER 7

| | Easy to grow | Can be potted | Light condition | Likes Compost | Height in feet | Flowers | Scent | Foliage |
|---|---|---|---|---|---|---|---|---|
| | | | | | | Noted for | | |
| **Plumeria Accuminata / Rubra** <br> Common Frangipani | ● | | ☼ | ● | 30 | ● | ● | |
| **Beaumontia Multiflora** | ● | | ☼ | ● | C | ● | | |
| **Dracaena Fragrans** | ● | ● | ☼ | ● | 25 | | | ● |
| **Cordyline Terminalis** | ● | ● | ☼ | ● | 4 | | | ● |
| **Polyscias or Panax** | ● | ● | ☼ | ● | 4 | | | ● |
| **Acalypha Godseffiana** | ● | ● | ☼ | ● | 8 | | | ● |
| **Exocaria** | ● | | ☼ | ● | 4 | | | ● |
| **Tecomaria Capensis** <br> Cape Honeysuckle | ● | ● | ☼ | ● | 6 | ● | | |
| **Persea Gratissima** <br> Avocado Pear | ● | | ☼ | ● | 40 | F | | |
| **Hibiscus Rosa-Sinensis** | ● | ● | ☼ | ● | 12 | ● | | |
| **Mesua Ferrea** <br> Ironwood Tree / Penaga | ● | | ☼ | ● | 60 | ● | ● | ● |
| **Lonicera Caprifolium** <br> Honeysuckle | ● | ● | ☼ | ● | C | ● | ● | |
| **Hibiscus Mutabilis** <br> Rose of Sharon | ● | ● | ☼ | ● | 8 | ● | | |
| **Pisonia Alba / Grandis** <br> Malayan Lettuce Tree | ● | | ☼ | ● | 15 | | | ● |

| C | Controllable creeper |
|---|---|
| C+ | Rampant creeper |
| F | Fruit |

| Plant | Easy to grow | Can be potted | Light condition | Likes Compost | Height in feet | Flowers | Scent | Foliage |
|---|:---:|:---:|:---:|:---:|:---:|:---:|:---:|:---:|
| **Ixora Coccinea** <br> Indian Ixora Group | • | • | ☀ | | 6 | • | | |
| **Ixora Javanica** <br> Javanese Ixora | • | • | ☼ | | 8 | • | | |
| **Acalypha Wilkesiana** <br> Beefsteak Plant | • | • | ☀ | • | 6 | | | • |
| **Caryota** <br> Fishtail Palm | • | • | ☀ | • | 20 | | | • |
| **Clerodendron Macrosiphon** <br> Witch's Tongue | • | • | ☀ | • | 3 | • | | |
| **Clerodendron Fragrans / Chinense** | • | • | ☼ | • | 5 | • | • | |
| **Schefflera Actinophylla** <br> Australian Ivy Palm / Umbrella Tree | • | • | ☀ | • | 10 | | | • |
| **Ardisia Eliptica** <br> Mata Pelandok / Ayam / Itek | • | | ☀ | • | 10 | | | • |
| **Bauhinia Kockiana** | • | • | ☼ | • | C | • | | |
| **Quisqualis Indica** <br> Rangoon Creeper / Drunken Sailor | • | • | ☀ | • | C+ | • | • | |
| **Pseuderanthemum Atropurpureum** | • | • | ☼ | • | 4 | | | • |
| **Haemanthus Multiflorus** <br> Sea Egg / Powder Puff | • | • | ☼ | • | 2 | • | | |
| **Tabernaemontana Corymbosa** <br> China Star Jasmine / Borneo Pinwheel | • | • | ☀ | | 6 | • | | |
| **Jatropha Pandurifolia** | • | • | ☀ | • | 8 | • | | |

| | Easy to grow | Can be potted | Light condition | Likes Compost | Height in feet | Noted for | | |
|---|---|---|---|---|---|---|---|---|
| | | | | | | Flowers | Scent | Foliage |
| C — Controllable creeper<br>C+ — Rampant creeper<br>F — Fruit | | | | | | | | |
| **Malvaviscus Arboreus Mexicanus**<br>Sleeping Hibiscus / Turk's Cap | • | | ☀ | • | 6 | • | | |
| **Duranta Repens renamed D. Erecta**<br>Golden Dewdrop | • | • | ☀ | • | 10 | • | | |

CHAPTER 8

| | Easy to grow | Can be potted | Light condition | Likes Compost | Height in feet | Flowers | Scent | Foliage |
|---|---|---|---|---|---|---|---|---|
| **Bambusa Glaucescens**<br>Bamboo | • | | ☀ | • | 12 | | | • |
| **Bambusa Variegata**<br>Variegated Bamboo | • | | ☀ | • | 12 | | | • |
| **Callistemon Lanceolotus / Citrinus**<br>Bottlebrush Tree | • | | ☀ | • | 30 | • | | • |
| **Dendrobrium Crumenatum**<br>Pigeon Orchid | • | | ☼ | | C | • | • | |
| **Asplenium Nidus**<br>Birds Nest Fern | • | | ☼ | | 3 | | | • |
| **Durio Zibenthenus**<br>Durian | • | | ☀ | • | 60 | F | | |
| **Scindapsus Pictus**<br>Money Plant | • | | ☼ | • | C+ | | | • |
| **Araucaria Cunninghamii**<br>Moreton Bay / Hoop Pine | • | | ☀ | • | 60 | | | • |
| **Roystonea Regia**<br>Royal Palm | • | | ☀ | • | 30 | | | • |
| **Passiflora Coccinea**<br>Red Passion Flower | • | | ☼ | • | C+ | • | | |
| **Congea Tomentosa**<br>Shower Orchid | • | | ☀ | • | C+ | • | | • |

| | C | Controllable creeper |
| --- | --- | --- |
| | C+ | Rampant creeper |
| | F | Fruit |

| | Easy to grow | Can be potted | Light condition | Likes Compost | Height in feet | Noted for — Flowers | Noted for — Scent | Noted for — Foliage |
| --- | --- | --- | --- | --- | --- | --- | --- | --- |
| **Petrea Volubilis** <br> Sandpaper Vine | ● | | ☀ | ● | C+ | ● | | |
| **Stenolobium / Tecoma Stans** <br> Yellow Bells | ● | | ☀ | | 10 | ● | | |
| **Mangifera Indica** <br> Mango | ● | | ☀ | ● | 30 | F | | |
| **Pandorea Jasminoides** <br> Bower Plant of Queensland | ● | ● | ☀ | ● | C | ● | | |
| **Mimusops Elengi** <br> Tanjong Tree | ● | | ☀ | ● | 30 | ● | ● | ● |
| **Gliricidia Sepium** <br> Mexican Lilac | ● | | ☀ | ● | 60 | ● | | |
| **Lithocarpus** | | | ☀ | ● | 60 | | | ● |
| **Ixora Sinensis** | ● | ● | ☀ | ● | 6 | ● | | |
| **Randia Macrantha** <br> Angels' Trumpets | ● | | ☀ | ● | 10 | ● | | |
| **Cordia Subcordata** <br> Sea Trumpet | | | ☀ | ● | 10 | ● | | |
| **Heliconia Humilis** <br> Lobster Claws | ● | | ☀ | ● | 6 | ● | | ● |
| **Ligustrum Sinense** <br> Chinese Privet | ● | | ☀ | ● | 6 | | | ● |
| **Rhapis Excelsa** <br> Rhapis Palm | ● | ● | ☀ | ● | 6 | | | ● |
| **Vanilla Fragrans** | | | ☀ | | C | ● | | |

| | | | | | | | | Noted for | | |
|---|---|---|---|---|---|---|---|---|---|---|
| **C** | Controllable creeper | | | | | | | | | |
| **C+** | Rampant creeper | | | | | | | | | |
| **F** | Fruit | | | | | | | | | |

| | Easy to grow | Can be potted | Light condition | Likes Compost | Height in feet | Flowers | Scent | Foliage |
|---|:---:|:---:|:---:|:---:|:---:|:---:|:---:|:---:|
| **CHAPTER 9** | | | | | | | | |
| **Michelia Alba** <br> White Chempaka Tree | ● | | ☀ | ● | 70 | ● | ● | ● |
| **Pinus Caribaea** <br> Caribbean Pine | ● | | ☀ | ● | 60 | | | ● |
| **Philodendron Creeper** | ● | | ☼ | ● | C+ | | | ● |
| **Dieffenbachia** | ● | ● | ☼ | ● | 5 | | | ● |
| Maidenhair Fern | ● | ● | ☷ | ● | 2 | | | ● |
| **Dracaena Surculosa** | ● | ● | ☼ | ● | 10 | | | ● |
| **Pandanus** <br> Pineapple family | ● | ● | ☼ | ● | 5 | | | ● |
| **Brunfelsia Americana** <br> Lady of the Night | | | ☼ | ● | 6 | ● | ● | |
| **Clerodendron Paniculata** <br> Pagoda Plant | ● | ● | ☼ | ● | 4 | ● | | |
| **Crinum Giganteum** <br> Java Lily | ● | ● | ☼ | ● | 4 | ● | ● | |
| **Bambusa Vulgaris** <br> Bamboo | ● | | ☀ | ● | 50 | | | ● |
| **Heliconia Psittacorum Lathispatha** | ● | ● | ☼ | ● | 4 | ● | | ● |
| **Strelitzia Reginae** <br> Bird of Paradise | | ● | ☀ | ● | 4 | ● | | |
| **Livistona Rotundifolia** <br> Fan Palm | ● | | ☼ | ● | 8 | | | ● |

| | | | | | | Noted for | | |
| Plant | Easy to grow | Can be potted | Light condition | Likes Compost | Height in feet | Flowers | Scent | Foliage |
|---|---|---|---|---|---|---|---|---|
| **Cyrtostachys Lakka** <br> Sealing Wax Palm / Pinang Raja | ● | | ☀ | ● | 15 | | | ● |
| **Triangular Palm** | | | ☼ | | 10 | | | ● |
| **Ptychosperma (Australian)** | ● | | ☼ | ● | 10 | | | ● |
| **Chrysalidocarpus** | ● | | ☀ | ● | 10 | | | ● |
| **Cocus Nucifera** <br> Coconut / Kelapa | ● | | ☀ | ● | 30 | F | | ● |
| **Pleomele Reflexa** | ● | | ☼ | ● | 10 | | | ● |
| **Cyperus Involucratus** <br> Umbrella Grass | ● | | ☀ | ● | 4 | | | ● |
| **Ficus Microcarpa** <br> Malayan Banyan Tree | | | ☀ | ● | 60 | | | ● |
| **Clerodendron Fragrans / Chinense** | ● | ● | ☼ | ● | 4 | ● | ● | |
| **Lagerstroemia Speciosa** <br> Rose of India / Queen's Flower | ● | | ☀ | ● | 30 | ● | | |
| **Hibiscus Schizopetalus** <br> Coral Hibiscus | ● | ● | ☀ | ● | 6 | ● | | |
| **Thunbergia Affinis** | ● | | ☀ | ● | 5 | ● | | |
| **Gardenia Jasminoides** <br> Cape Jasmine | ● | ● | ☀ | ● | 10 | ● | ● | |
| **Cassia Fistula** <br> Indian Laburnum | ● | | ☀ | ● | 40 | ● | | |

C    Controllable creeper
C+   Rampant creeper
F    Fruit

| | Easy to grow | Can be potted | Light condition | Likes Compost | Height in feet | Noted for | | |
|---|---|---|---|---|---|---|---|---|
| | | | | | | Flowers | Scent | Foliage |
| **C** Controllable creeper **C+** Rampant creeper **F** Fruit | | | | | | | | |
| **Delonix Regia** Flame of the Forest | • | | ☼ | • | 40 | • | | |
| **Ipomomea Learii** Morning Glory | • | • | ☼ | • | C+ | • | | |
| | | | | | | | | |

## CHAPTER 10

| | Easy to grow | Can be potted | Light condition | Likes Compost | Height in feet | Flowers | Scent | Foliage |
|---|---|---|---|---|---|---|---|---|
| **Spathodea Campanulata** African Tulip Tree | • | | ☼ | • | 60 | • | | |
| **Cassia Multijuga** | • | | ☼ | • | 50 | • | | |
| **Carica Papaya** Papaya Tree | • | | ☼ | • | 10 | F | | |
| **Limau Kesturi** Musk Lime | • | • | ☼ | • | 6 | F | | |
| **Gardenia Tubifera** Water Gardenia Tree | • | | ☼ | • | 30 | • | • | |
| **Gardenia Carinata** Kedah Gardenia | • | | ☼ | • | 30 | • | • | |
| **Canna Orientalis** Scarlet Canna | • | • | ☼ | • | 3 | • | | |
| **Phaeomeria Speciosa** Torch Ginger / Kantan | • | • | ◑ | • | 10 | • | | |
| **Pandanus Amaryllifolius** Pandan | • | • | ◑ | • | 2 | | | • |
| **Cerbera Odollam** Pong Pong Tree | • | | ☼ | • | 30 | • | • | |
| **Golden Banana** Pisang Mas | • | | ☼ | • | 10 | F | | |

C   Controllable creeper
C+  Rampant creeper
F   Fruit

| | Easy to grow | Can be potted | Light condition | Likes Compost | Height in feet | Noted for | | |
|---|---|---|---|---|---|---|---|---|
| | | | | | | Flowers | Scent | Foliage |
| **Fagraea Fragrans** <br> Tembusu Tree | ● | | ☀ | | 60 | ● | ● | |
| **Maingaya Malayana** | | | ☀ | ● | 20 | | | ● |
| **Tonkin Creeper** <br> Telosma Cordata | ● | ● | ☀ | ● | C | ● | ● | |

CHAPTER 11

| | Easy to grow | Can be potted | Light condition | Likes Compost | Height in feet | Flowers | Scent | Foliage |
|---|---|---|---|---|---|---|---|---|
| **Bougainvillea** <br> Paper flower / Bunga Kertas | ● | ● | ☀ | ● | 5 | ● | | |
| **Epiphyllum Oxypetalum** <br> Queen of the Night / Keng Hua | ● | ● | ☼ | ● | 2 | ● | ● | |
| **Adenium Coetanum** <br> Desert Rose | ● | ● | ☀ | ● | 4 | ● | | |
| **Euphorbia Splendens** <br> Crown of Thorns | ● | ● | ☀ | ● | 4 | ● | | |
| **Caladium** | ● | ● | ☼ | ● | 2 | | | ● |
| **Anthurium** | ● | ● | ☼ | ● | 2 | | | ● |
| **Plumeria Obtusa** | ● | | ☀ | ● | 40 | ● | ● | |
| **Erythrina Orientalis (formerly Indica)** <br> Indian Coral Tree / Tiger's Claw / Dadap | ● | | ☀ | ● | 20 | ● | | |
| **Pseudocalymma Alliaceum** <br> Garlic Vine | ● | ● | ☀ | ● | C | ● | | |
| **Stephanotis Floribunda** <br> Madagascar Jasmine | | | ☀ | C | ● | ● | | |

| | Easy to grow | Can be potted | Light condition | Likes Compost | Height in feet | Noted for | | |
| --- | --- | --- | --- | --- | --- | --- | --- | --- |
| | | | | | | Flowers | Scent | Foliage |
| C — Controllable creeper | | | | | | | | |
| C+ — Rampant creeper | | | | | | | | |
| F — Fruit | | | | | | | | |
| **Murraya Paniculata** <br> Mock Orange / Kemuning | • | | ☀ | • | 15 | • | • | |
| **Alamanda Cathartica** | • | • | ☀ | • | 4 | • | | |
| **Solandra Nitida** <br> Chalice Vine | • | | ☀ | • | C+ | • | | |
| **Wrightea Religiosa** | • | • | ☀ | • | 5 | • | • | |
| **Jasminum Sambac** <br> Arabian Jasmine | • | • | ☀ | • | 3 | • | • | |
| **Brunfelsia Pauciflora Floribunda** <br> Yesterday, Today & Tomorrow | • | • | ☀ | • | 10 | • | • | |
| **Chempaka Figo** <br> Dwarf Chempaka | • | • | ☀ | • | 8 | • | • | |
| **Cananga Odorata / Dwarf Kenanga** <br> Ylang-Ylang | • | • | ☀ | • | 10 | • | • | |
| **Mussaenda Philippica** | • | • | ☀ | • | 10 | • | | |
| **Melia Indica** <br> Nim Tree | • | | ☀ | • | 40 | | | • |

# Index

Illustrations in italics

| | Text Page | Reference Guide |
|---|---|---|
| Cocus Nucifera | 68 | 101 |
| Common Frangipani p. 16 | 47 | 96 |
| Congea Tomentosa | 60 | 98 |
| Coral Hibiscus | 70 | 101 |
| Cordia Subcordata | 63 | 99 |
| Cordyline Terminalis | 49 | 96 |
| Crinum Giganteum | 67 | 100 |
| Crown of Thorns | 86 | 103 |
| Cyperus Involucratus p. 73 | 69 | 101 |
| Cyrtostachys Lakka | 68 | 101 |
| **D** | | |
| Dadap p. 64 | 87 | 103 |
| Delonix Regia p. 6 | 69 | 102 |
| Dendrobrium Crumenatum p. 56 | 57 | 98 |
| Desert Rose | 86 | 103 |
| Dieffenbachia | 67 | 100 |
| Dracaena Fragrans | 49 | 96 |
| Dracaena Surculosa | 67 | 100 |
| Drunken Sailor p. 44 | 54 | 97 |
| Duranta Repens | | |
| renamed Duranta Erecta p. 55 | 55 | 98 |
| Durio Zibenthenus | 59 | 98 |
| Durian | 59 | 98 |
| Dwarf Chempaka | 90 | 104 |
| Dwarf Kenanga p. 84, 78 | 90 | 104 |
| **E** | | |
| Epiphyllum Oxypetalum p. 35 | 86 | 103 |
| Erythrina Orientalis p. 64 | 87 | 103 |
| Euphorbia Splendens | 86 | 103 |
| Exocaria | 50 | 96 |
| **F** | | |
| Fagraea Fragrans | 79 | 102 |
| Fan Palm | 68 | 100 |
| Ficus Microcarpa | 69 | 101 |
| Fishtail Palm | 52, 68 | 97 |
| Flame of the Forest p. 6 | 69 | 102 |
| **G** | | |
| Gardenia Carinata | 76 | 102 |
| Gardenia Jasminoides | 70 | 101 |
| Gardenia Tubifera p. 53 | 76 | 102 |
| Garlic Vine p. 71 | 87 | 103 |
| Gliricidia Sepium | 61 | 99 |
| Golden Banana | 79 | 102 |
| Golden Dewdrop p. 55 | 55 | 98 |
| **H** | | |
| Haemanthus Multiflorus p. 74 | 54 | 97 |
| Heliconia Humilis | 63 | 99 |
| Heliconia Psittacorum | | |
| Lathispatha | 67 | 100 |
| Hibiscus Mutabilis | 51 | 96 |
| Hibiscus Rosa-Sinensis p. 22 | 50 | 96 |
| Hibiscus Schizopetalus | 70 | 101 |
| Honeysuckle | 51 | 96 |
| Hoop Pine | 60 | 98 |
| **I** | | |
| Indian Coral Tree p. 64 | 87 | 103 |

*Illustrations in italics*

AMERICAN QUARTER

GATE

THE HOUSE

FRENCH QUARTER

TERRACE

N